Dethroning the Systemic Patriarchal Social System

A New Dawn for the Environment and Human Rights

By: Daniel Paul Woodring

ISBN: 9781734017212

First print edition 2020

Also available as an eBook from Kindle Direct Publishing

Dedication

**To all who have been stifled by
The Systemic Patriarchal Social System**

**A New Dawn is coming for the environment
with
Respect, dignity, and equal rights for all humanity**

Table of Contents

Forward

I first met Dan Woodring in 1992, when we were both selected to be part of a citizens' group charged with developing a twenty-year vision for our local community. Dan went on to co-chair that group when it was reassembled ten years later to keep our momentum going. That community, West Chester, Ohio has gone on to become Money Magazine's Best Place to Live in Ohio and among the top 40 communities to live and raise a family in the entire United States. In the interim, I have worked personally with Dan, who served as my life coach as I sought purpose and meaning after successfully selling a business I'd grown for more than fifteen years. Dan deserves no small measure of credit for the direction my life has taken because of the sincere interest he took in guiding me.

Dan now seeks to tackle a much larger and challenging subject – the United States of America, and the world at large. One hardly needs to be convinced that we are at a very troubling point in our nation's history – a crossroads, really – where the path we choose will quite likely determine the fate, and possibly the survival, of our country as we know it. In "Dethroning the Systemic Patriarchal Social System", Dan argues convincingly that not only is God everywhere, but that God is of and part of each of us. We thus have the power within to effect the change needed to right our troubled ship. Dan's unique insights and observations lead to a prescription that calls upon us to rebalance how we manifest the divine within each of us.

This book stays away from dogma. Instead, it explores the underlying causes for many of the conflicting themes that have plagued Man's search for universal truth that can be found in the contradictory "eye-for-an-eye" retribution of the Old Testament and "turn-the-other-cheek" tolerance of the New. These contradictions are common across faiths – Christianity, Judaism and Islam all struggle with these dichotomies. In his book, Dan suggests a unique explanation for these contradictions and that our current state of affairs is due to an imbalance that for too long has favored one view over the other.

It must be reiterated that this book does not argue faith, dogma or scripture. In fact, it explicitly and doggedly avoids those topics, seeking instead to discuss universal truth that has much to do with what I personally see as Einstein's theory of relativity (E=MC^2) at its very essence, where everything is part of a universal energy. And just as Einstein's equation is an elegant balance of mass and energy, so does Dan seek to balance and rebalance the equation of how that energy is applied to our daily interactions with each other and with ourselves as we seek peace, love, success and happiness. "Dethroning the Systemic Patriarchal Social System" works as both an instructional insight to how universal truths apply in both our personal lives and the world at large, and as a roadmap to help us choose the proper path as we sit at this crossroads in history. It is an important work at a critical time.

Paul Szydlowski

2020 - The Perfect Storm

So, we see, we perceive, we feel the tension. The world and our human/collective consciousness is in an epic crisis. The energy of the world system is so critically unbalanced we are experiencing the consciousness system delivering a major self-correcting storm. I invite you to pause a moment and consciously visualize the darkness of the storm. Let it sink in ... be aware of the perfect storm of 2020:

> Climate crises
> Covid-19 Pandemic
> Systemic racism – civil unrest at a high
> Systemic misogyny – being called out
> Discriminatory practices being challenged –
> human rights for women, blacks,
> > LGBTQ communities, and minorities – all
> > those being disenfranchised
> Fight against voter suppression and oppression
> Political disfunction – polarization; lack of
> > Administrative and Congressional
> > leadership
> Socioeconomic disparity causing major societal
> > disturbances.
> Economic recession
> Waring conflicts and nuclear threats
> Healthcare crises
> Moral and spiritual deterioration
> Systemic patriarchal system – power, dominance,
> and control causing major distresses; approaching
> > pure fascism by some

When we look at the social consciousness of the world it is obvious, we are still living in a primitive society. We are going through some tough times and what we do not realize is we are moving along on an evolutionary path that has us transitioning to a new social order. We are awakening. What we are really experiencing is the pain when there is a seismic shift in consciousness. To me, this is positive, and that is exciting. Be at peace and get ready to be a part of this historic life journey. Do your part and realize ….

Out of chaos will come order

Preface

Dethroning the Systemic Patriarchal Social System
A New Dawn for the Environment and Human Rights

By: Daniel Woodring

We all have a sense of the troubled world in which we live. We talk about it, but it is difficult to get a handle on the situation, and even more difficult to zero in on the cause(s) and solutions. So, just what is the state of the World Consciousness today? To help us "see" and feel the state of our world consciousness, let us draw a metaphorical picture taken by an extraterrestrial enlightened source:

Extraterrestrial Metaphor

Advanced extraterrestrial beings – aliens - from another galaxy are on a quest to explore other worlds in search for a suitable place to expanded colonization. One team was given the assignment to travel to a planet called Earth to do a review of the planetary conditions or consciousness, and report back as to the suitability. Here is their report:

> *"The earth is a troubled world. There is overwhelming consciousness of negativity existing in earthlings. There is much hatred, violence, and separateness; many of its peoples live in poverty; famine and disease, many with health issues, while others live in opulence.*
>
> *Their airways are filled with negative vibrations coming from human thoughts and beliefs, violent and destructive programming from TV's, radio, and video gaming depicting hate, violence, separation, bias, and bigotry. They are obsessed 24/7 with mass digital pollution.*

They know not of their oneness. Racial bias, antisemitism, ethnic and cultural bias, bigotry, and gender inequity separate them and keep them from living the peace that is available to them. They live in ignorance of the spiritual realm and thus know not who they are: spiritual beings that have chosen to have a human experience on their planet.

Crazy things are happening in their environment. The environment is screaming. The system is way out of balance with floods, fires, water quality and dirty air putting the planet and population in jeopardy. Animals, vegetation, and air quality are suffering immensely. They fail to see the interconnectedness of all things.

One of the human population areas called The United States is in the process of an election of a leader they call President. There is no spiritual focus in the process and the earthlings are bound up in hate, divisiveness, and separation. Big government, big business, big pharmacy, are forcing more separation while the suffering of individual humans is increasing.

Practice of White Nationalism, White Supremacy, racism, ethnic cleansing, antisemitism, racial profiling, – bigotry of all kinds, is keeping them in bondage, and they seem ignorant and unaware of how this is affecting the world consciousness and thus their lives.

Their world is polarized and separated in mind and spirit. Hawkish waring nations are posing nuclear threats on each other; they are in the midst of economic globalization but are hindered by cultural bias, trade wars, social and economic posturing, and wars. There are some good things going on, but the negative consciousness persists and is growing.

They are ignorant or unaware of who they truly are and the power of their being, and fail to see the world as a sacred, living, breathing organism with the interconnection of all things. They are all ONE but do not know it or live it.

On top of all this, they are in the midst of a virus outbreak they call Covid-19. With all this happening they are experiencing a "perfect storm" - their energy system rebelling to self-correct the energy disturbance of the perfect storm.

Most of the people on the planet are living in a primitive social system we might call a Systemic Patriarchal Monarchy. They do not realize it, but it is the cause of most of the problems we have witnessed including their COVID virus. There needs to be a serious intervention and a transformation to an "enlightened" social system.

Team Leader: this does not sound good. Are they worth saving or should we move on to another planetary system?

Yes, they are worth it, but an intervention is necessary to reverse the negative downward spiral and save them from themselves. Saving the earth would be a huge blessing to the totality of planet and interstellar system. They need rescued from themselves and we think that can be done. Our intervention will be to assist in the seismic shift in world consciousness – a shift from negative human thought energy to the spiritual energy of The Divine Feminine. In doing so, the energy system of the earth will come back into balance and become a peaceful, heavenly paradise for all living things, and a stellar example to the universe. It will take a massive awakening of the earthlings, but we think it can be done and they have what it takes.

Okay then, LET'S GO FOR IT!

Join me in this awakening journey!

Introduction

Dethroning the Systemic Patriarchal Social System
A New Dawn for the Environment and Human Rights

The Preface – the extraterrestrial metaphor, paints a dim picture of the state of the world in which we live. Yet, this is an exciting time to be alive. I say that in the face of the title, "Dethroning the Systemic Patriarchal Social System". We are talking about a seismic shift in our social system and our world consciousness energy system. That will not necessarily be fun or easy. Why a shift, and a shift to what? We will be talking about the attributes of The Divine Feminine, a spiritual consciousness we must awaken to and embrace. To sort this all out we must understand the evolution of what is going on in world consciousness today at a deep level, both physically and spiritually, and how we got to where we are. This will explain why a shift in world consciousness is necessary. The question is, what happens if we do not, and how to make the shift – if we choose to do so?

When I initially thought of and then expressed my desire and the need for such a book, there were those around me who questioned my qualifications. Let me share with you. First, the need is obvious, but why me? My true sense is that writing this book is the next phase of my Soul Contract for this incarnation. The qualifications came with all the necessary talents, skills, and life knowledge along with the experiences that would lead to the manifestation of this manuscript. Let me explain further.

As far back as I can remember I have been in search of answers to the big questions; who am I, why am I here? Am I the person in this body or something deeper and more profound? What is my mission and purpose in life? Is there a God, and who is She? Where is She, and why does She allow all this evil and suffering we see in our world today? Where is She in all this? We are all on a journey and what I have learned is that most all of us have these same questions and are searching in our own way for answers.

Along my journey I have had several significant life change markers that extensively broadened my view of reality. The first came after completing my BME and MBA degrees and working in business. I discovered that most businesses, including the one I was working for, do a poor job at planning. I was taught the key to success is to plan your work and then work your plan. Going down the rabbit hole I realized that this same scenario is true for how most of us "lead" our lives. As a result of this experience, I began to think more deeply about the personal implications of planning to my life. I wondered about things like: who am I, why am I here, what is my personal vision, mission, and purpose for my life: What is mine to do? What do I really want to do in life that would allow me the leave this world with no regrets? If I discovered what is mine to do, how would I do it, what would it look like, what skills and "attitude" shifts would I need? The search led me to developing the material for my first book, *"No Regrets, A Comprehensive Guide and Workbook for Mapping Your Life's Journey Regardless of Age"*, self-published in 2003. This was obviously a tool developed for me. In addition to the book came my mission statement for my life, *"Helping Individuals and Organizations Reach Potential"*. I was the first client. In addition to the planning aspects, the research and study put into writing the "No Regrets" workbook came with a deeper awakening or discovery of who I am and why I am the way I am. It also came with a better understanding of God, spirituality, consciousness, belief systems, and the role of intentions and thinking in our lives. One of the biggest epiphanies was a deep realization that *who I am is a spiritual being having a human experience*, not a human being that once in a while have a spiritual experience. This was also the time that I shifted living my life from a religious base to a spiritual base.

Another major growth marker and experience for me was the study and research for my second book, *"Genesis 2.0 – Science Redefining Spirituality"*, published in 2019 through Kindle Direct. In writing the book I finally arrived at a deep knowing and understanding of the who and what of God, what true reality is, and the many states of consciousness including the collective consciousness. This was huge for me. To cap things off, while researching and development of the chapter on spiritual practices, I came to grips with what was necessary to raise my human consciousness and connect more easily with a higher dimension. The experience gave me the ability to "see" the world situation with an unobstructed view. It was almost like the Universe saying, "Okay, Dan, here is some knowledge I want you to share with the world". The book became part of my life plan.

From my study and research for "Genesis 2.0", I must share some critical truths I learned, and emphasize some important focus points that will help us through the maze of the world energy disaster we find ourselves in.

- God is Pure Consciousness, an all pervasive, all-powerful, creative and intelligent energy field everywhere present – an all-knowing field of energy that holds everything together. It is THE ENERGY SYSTEM of the universe, and everything that exists in the Material State -or any state of existence is part of this energy field. It is the source of all life which expresses in all three states of existence, and we/It are part of it – THE ONE – with no separation, no duality.

- Know who you are!!! We do not have a Spirit – we are Spirit with spiritual superpowers – power, genius, and creativity, available and awaiting our activation and use. Who we are is Spirit having a human experience. That means we are all individualized centers of consciousness in the God Energy Consciousness System. I am God expressing as me, you are God expressing as you.

- Within each of us humans exists two forms of consciousness – Spiritual Consciousness and Human Consciousness. Although they are distinct but both part of the grand consciousness system we call God or Pure Consciousness. There is no separation. We are ONE mind, body Spirit consciousness with no beginning or end. Death only comes to the body which for our lifetime on this planet is the house for our spirit or soul to express God on this earth plane. There is no death to Spirit – life continues through eternity.

- Thought energy is the most powerful form of energy there is. Thought is the causal force behind the material world. As we think, so we and our world is/become. Every thought is essentially a "prayer" that is lifted into the consciousness realm, mirrored back, and produce effects, good or bad, depending on what we send "up". So, what we as a species experience in life – and that includes all the negative stuff we see today, is a result of our collective consciousness that is reflecting back. The good news is as we shift our thinking based on the Divine - the Spirit within, love and peace prosper. Thus, *A Seismic Shift in Human Consciousness – The Rise of The Divine Feminine" is* an awakening we must all strive for.

There were many more experiences that have led me along the way, but one that touched me deeply is the 7 years I served as a hospital chaplain. Here I learned, with a high degree of equanimity, and my training to be loving, compassionate, understanding, and empathetic, to assist patients not only with their spiritual needs but their physical needs. In doing this I became highly aware of the false and negative programming we have all endured. For example, while helping patients through end of life situations, I often heard their fear of death had to do with their mental programming of *"I am not worthy, I have sinned and will not go to heaven, God doesn't love me, I have been too bad, I don't deserve heaven, it is God's will that I suffer"* – and more. It made me aware of the millions upon millions of humans that have belief systems based on fear, lies, false information and programming ... a collective consciousness that has put them in a mind prison which has put severe limitations on life. I decided that part of my soul contract is to find the truth and educate as many as possible to the truth that we are Spirit Beings with unlimited potential and have the wisdom, intelligence, and power to be all that we can be. In this realization, I revised my personal mission statement to *"Helping Individuals and Organizations Awaken to and Fully Live Their Essence"*. I am hopeful that writing this book helps me achieve my mission and soul contract.

As we look at the world today, we realize most of us live in mediocrity, in some sort of self-prison and are severely self-limited. we are bombarded with stories and events that would seem to demonstrate the ignorance of Spirit aspects of life. We appear as a people on this planet that are asleep, not awakened, drowning in negativizes, separated and not aware of our divinity. Yet we know there are awakened, intelligent, spirit filled people, they just do not make front page news. Why? Because most of us are programmed to watch the negative stuff. As my dad would say, negative sells newspapers. As a result, 87% to 90% of our programmed consciousness, our operating system for life is negative. This fact has led us to a world or collective consciousness that has taken us to the brink of disaster.

It is not an accident that you and I were born in these times. Know it or not, we all have been "called up" to address this unique opportunity to rally and change our world and consciousness for the positive, or, face perhaps the sixth mass distinction of the world as we know it. This is a huge undertaking and to me, that is exciting. As the alien search team delegation said, our world does not have to be like it is, and we have the power, tools, and intelligence to bring the energy system of the world back into balance and become a peaceful, heavenly paradise for all.

Dethrone the Systemic Patriarchal Social System

We are all trying to make sense of what is going on in our world. We see and feel the tenseness, and It seems that every segment of society is wheeling with fear, trepidation, and anxiety. Truly, the energy system of the world is crazily out of balance. We are about to go on a discovery journey to find out why and provide some solutions.

First off and right up front, I want to set up the predominant probable cause of most of the world crisis that is causing the disturbance and imbalance in the collective consciousness system. That most probable cause is – **the systemic patriarchal social system in which we live.** In building a case for this rationale as the cause we will need to thoroughly understand the terms "patriarchy", "collective consciousness" and "energy systems" of the world, along with the "Divine Feminine" which will portray the values by which we can and should be living to bring order back from chaos to live in a peaceful enlightened state. Once we understand these terms, we will apply this knowledge and perspective to the energy disturbances and fragmentation we see manifest in the environment along with the resulting ugliness we see as systemic misogyny, systemic racism, socioeconomic disparity, and other energy disturbances such as viruses. The common denominator in all these disturbance is the systemic patriarchal social system. When we finish the journey, I believe the conclusion will be obvious. We must dethrone the systemic patriarchal social system.

Let us start the discussion with the term **Patriarchy.** According to Wikipedia, "patriarchy is a social system in which men hold primary power and (are) predominate in roles of political leadership, moral authority, social privilege and control of property". It is generally accepted that most contemporary societies are patriarchal in nature. Over time, a patriarchal system can become so strong and dominate that male "leaders" holding the power in the society naturally progress to the domination, oppression, and exploitation of not only women, but "others" that are "different" – races and ethnicities, all of which automatically enforces and encourages and leads to social stratification. The system becomes "systemic" – engrained and universal in its application. Perhaps you can begin to see what has happened to our world.

So, For over thousands of years, human consciousness, The Collective Unconscious, has been programmed with a behavior and belief that men, male energy, and women, female energy are separate and distinct. And since the system – us, believed and acted accordingly, it became true in our illusionary reality. Over time, this belief gradually manifest itself into what we see today, a systemic system where patriarchal energy dominates. We live in a world adrift in a sea of dominant masculine energy, and it is becoming progressively toxic. This heightened patriarchal culture has saddled us with a social system with the predominant masculine qualities of dominance, control, and power. This has been projected as men are better than, stronger and more deserving than women and "others". This has cast a picture of women and "others" as subservient, less than, and not as worthy. This has consciously and unconsciously perpetuated the massive systemic energy imbalances we are experiencing today. Our patriarchal system has drowned out the feminine qualities of compassion, empathy and nurturing, all energies so desperately needed for communal society. This is one reason we will be talking about The Rise of The Divine Feminine as a necessity to return our system to balance.

The conclusion we are heading for is we need to dethrone the systemic patriarchal social system and replace it with what I will call an "enlightened" social system with needed spiritual qualities that will bring a new dawn for the environment and respect, dignity, and equal rights for all humanity. Now that is a journey worth taking. We will be developing a thesis on how to dethrone the systemic patriarchal system while providing the basic structure of a new system we will call the **"Enlightened Social System"**. Enjoy the journey!

Dethrone the Systemic Patriarchal System Ideology

The Divine Feminine

I have included this chapter up front so we can realize that what we are experiencing in the world today is the beginning of a seismic shift in world consciousness. We may not realize it, but it is a spiritual movement. What I have discovered in my life and research is that all of existence is energy. All the material world, you, me, our thoughts – it is all energy. As covered in the Introduction, all of this is part of the God Conscious System. We will be talking about the lack of balance in the world energy system bringing us to 2020 and the perfect storm. A great part of the world energy imbalance is the current dominance of toxic male energy. The shift in consciousness we are seeing is due in part by a rise of female energy. But, it is more than this. In reality we are experiencing a rise in spiritual energy and the need for more of the divine feminine energy to emerge to balance the forces. Thus, the discussion about the divine feminine in the totality of God Energy.

The Rise of the Divine Feminine. This statement comes with many questions. What does that really mean? Why are we even talking about God's gender? How is this going to help us out of the quagmire in which we find ourselves? How does this relate to the world consciousness? So, we have some searching and discovery to do, but in the end, it will make sense. First, we must come to an acceptable definition of God, to lead us to some answers. Most of us accept that God is not gender specific, although we often refer to God as Father. My favorite surname is Mother-Father God, but in text I refer to God as She or Her. I will explain why in a moment.

In my book "Genesis 2.0 – Science Redefining Spirituality" I arrived at this definition of God:

God is Pure Consciousness, the All-pervasive universal quantum field of energy – a cosmic being with infinite power, intelligence, and Love that is everywhere present. God is all there is. God is the totality of all states of existence, and we are one with and an integral part of the flow of this God Consciousness – this God Energy.

This definition of God is much too scientific for most of us and therefore tough to connect with. So, let us go back to what we do know, what we feel comfortable with and the current programming in the minds of most people. This translates into:

God is infinite Love, Power, Intelligence and Compassion. God is Life, Truth, Beauty, Consciousness, True Reality, Absolute Oneness, Divine Presence and Spirit. God is The Universe. God is all there is.

God is all there is. Therefore, She is the totality of Feminine and Masculine – no separation. And since you and I are Spirit, ONE with God, you and I have the full attributes of the Divine Feminine and Masculine within us – no separation, except in our mind we call our human consciousness. Therein lies the problem.

To understand what is being said here we need a quick review. Within each of us humans exists two forms of consciousness – Spiritual Consciousness and Human Consciousness. There is no separation, we are ONE – mind, body, spirit – consciousness with no beginning or end. We don't have a Spirit, we are Spirit with spiritual superpowers – power, genius, and creativity available and awaiting our activation and disposal. We have two truth's here: we are this essence and have a life purpose, to awaken to this power and live life fully. The trouble is most of us are living only from our human consciousness. The evolution of this consciousness in the world has become toxic. The message of the man Jesus several thousand years ago was – hey, wake up, start using the Spirit within to run your life and you will experience the kingdom. Of course there have been many other profits and spiritual systems with the same message. Unfortunately, we have continued to live in a hypnotic human trance state. Although we are living from a primitive mindset, the exciting thing is we are beginning to awaken. It is a spiritual awakening that will put us in touch with who we truly are, spiritual beings, with the power to live rich full lives "in the kingdom" which is already here. We just don't see it. That is where the divine feminine and masculine come in. We need to get in touch with that.

Here is what I am saying. In 2020 we are experiencing the crescendo of what happens when there is total negligence in expressing our spiritual being. In particular, we are experiencing a limited amount of the feminine qualities from our spirit being. When this happens, like the culture of the 21st century, the patriarchal system – our human consciousness, takes over and we are prone to physical and mental diseases, intolerant to differences, power grabbing, racists, bigots, impatient with the pace of growth, and losing the Divine Feminine values of love, kindness, patience, flexibility and goodness.

The key is awakening to the fact that we are spirit beings, an instrument through which God manifests. If we are connected and conscious, that manifestation can be a powerful combination of all of God's qualities, balanced so that we can experience the heaven on earth that spiritual scholars talk about. This will only happen if we are connected to Spirit, conscious of our true nature.

For all of us, this is a wake-up call. A seismic or tectonic shift in human consciousness must take place so that we awaken to and fully live and use the power of our essence. We must realize and act in our knowing that it takes a balance of the qualities of both the Divine Feminine and Divine Masculine energies to create peace and harmony and to provide the solutions we all need to save our world.

So, we now know that there is no separation in divine energies. It is all one Energy, Consciousness, neither exclusively masculine nor feminine in nature. Some may not like it, but if we are to correct the imbalance of energy in our world and reach our destiny we must accept the fact that as spirit beings we have both the feminine and masculine within us – no separation – and it is high time we release and express the feminine part of us. It can no longer be ignored. Now, for purposes of bringing us to the point of better understanding and demonstration of the need for a seismic shift in world consciousness, we will use human understanding of feminine and masculine to clarify our points and give us direction. When we say "Rise of the Divine Feminine" we are talking about an awakening and better utilization of the feminine qualities of Spirit, balanced with the masculine in our world. Understanding starts with understanding of terms.

Feminine energy – an energy that is typically characteristic and attributable to females of our species and includes: love, nurturing, caring, pleasing, joy, compassion, empathy, tolerance, decency, engagement, collaboration and listening.

Masculine energy - an energy that is typically characteristic and attributable to males of our species and includes: dominant, aggressive, assertion, directive, and control.

Divine Feminine: the expression of the feminine qualities of spiritual consciousness. Whenever you express God through you as love, peace, grace, compassion, empathy, and tolerance - qualities or characteristics normally attributable to the feminine gender, you are demonstrating the Divine Feminine. What we are trying to get across here is that the Divine Feminine does not have as much to do with gender as it does a state of consciousness – a way of thinking and being.

For centuries, women have been defined by the men around them, so first we need to restore the power to them – literally and psychologically. That means consciously elevating women to positions of power and leadership, returning a more nurturing, compassionate, empathetic, and understanding consciousness to our world. To make this work, women must also project some of the qualities within them associated with the divine masculine. At the same time, since we are looking for feminine/masculine energy balance, we need a healthy mix and interplay of feminine energy with masculine energy, but for men, a masculine energy that is still there but softened to include feminine qualities. This will require men in our society to back down and at the same time step up. Imagine a world with all its people having full access to the energy of both the Divine Feminine and Divine Masculine. Finding balance between apparent opposites is a multifaceted undertaking but will be empowering and enlightening to our world.

Let us start at the beginning. Because of a predominately patriarchal society of the world culture for thousands of years, and as a result, world consciousness, the divine feminine qualities or spiritual consciousness has been largely suppressed, blocking the total flow of God Energy, both feminine and masculine. So when we say, "Rise of the Divine Feminine – Needed: a "Seismic-Shift in Human Consciousness", we are talking about consciously reintroducing or embodying the societal system with behavior that is as much feminine as masculine. We need a balance of these energies.

Today there is a need for greater expression of feminine characteristics in world leadership. That means changing the expectations for leaders personally, professional, and politically. That means moving away from drive, power, and directive management to understanding, cooperation, empathy, compassion, tolerance, collaboration, listening and teamwork. It needs to be a blend of masculine and feminine.

The concept of this book is to balance the world energy/consciousness system through rise of the divine feminine. Imagine people exploring consciousness in way that invites them to become more balanced, compassionate, and altruistic and appreciative of differences. This means becoming more oriented toward caring about the welfare and rights of others, feeling concern and empathy, and acting in ways that build up the whole of humanity.

In the end it is not about the divine feminine or divine masculine, it is about a spiritual awakening that connects us to the Divine to liberate us from suffering, lack, and limitation, and restores human dignity to the rightful place. Again, the reason we are emphasizing the divine feminine now is because for thousands of years there has been a gross imbalance in the energy system that has negated the feminine qualities needed in our world to avert disaster of the 6th mass extinction. It is that serious.

As we restore the masculine and feminine (spiritual) balance, we will see a shift in world consciousness that is open to "seeing" and experiencing heaven on earth. We each must do our part.

What we will be bringing into the light are ways to become aware of our energy imbalance and free us of the cultural programming hypnosis we are living. Time to break out of prison and rise above our victim mentality.

As we embark on this journey, realize there are many energy systems active in our world today that are unbalanced and so much of it because of the feminine/masculine energy imbalance. This is causing the collective unconscious of humanity to darken, thicken, and grow increasingly negative. It all has to do with the way we humans - primarily the masculine traits - have been treating the earth and each other.

The consciousness of human thought, behavior, and action have seriously put a negative spin on the environment which is the consciousness of nature. In addition, human thought, action, and behavior has distressed the collective consciousness through the foolish commission of violent acts like world conflicts and wars. And finally, over the centuries, humans have developed cultural systems with rules, laws, policies, techniques, and practices that have totally violated the dignity of humans and their rights as children of the ONE. Racism and ethnic-based discrimination is widespread. An unbalanced socioeconomic stratification has produced pervasive inequalities in income, housing, health care, employment, education, and economic opportunity. Sickness and disease is disproportionately an encumbrance of the "have nots". In short, the world energy system and the consciousness that drives life on this planet is seriously out of balance. It is time for *The Rise of the Divine Feminine* for a seismic shift in the Collective Consciousness.

Awaken
Spirit Is the Healing And Binding Force For All Existence

Everything is Energy

It is All Energy – All Things in the Universe and beyond – Everything - is Energy – And The World Energy System is Out of Balance -

If you look up the definition of energy, you will find something like this: Energy is a property of and object or system (particle); a vibrational force of an object or system; a subatomic activity – a force or property of moving electrons. So, although we do not know exactly what "energy" is, we know what it can do and how it behaves. Electricity is a good example of this. The next step of understanding for me was one of the most exciting and fascinating things I learned in engineering physics class - the law of conservation of energy, which states that everything we see and touch on the physical plane is energy. In addition, science taught us and has proven that we can neither create nor destroy energy – BUT – we can change its "form" from one state to another. This is one of the premises Einstein used in developing his theory of relativity. All the above just relates to energy on the physical state of existence. How about energy in the Spiritual and Quantum states of existence?

With my background as an engineer and with my study and research for my book "Genesis 2.0", I have come to understand existence from the standpoint that it all begins and ends with energy, and that this energy can and does transcend one state to another. It is all energy, just in different forms. Simply stated, God is energy, we are energy, our spirit is energy, thought is energy, and consciousness is energy. For example, prayer and meditation are practices that raise our consciousness (energy) to connect directly into the higher frequencies of energy in different states. The concept is simple, but it is a bit difficult to comprehend. However, having a good feel for this energy concept is critical to understanding what the collective consciousness is, how it got into the current state, and why a radical shift in the collective consciousness is necessary to avoid a catastrophe.

So, here is the way it is. We know that all existence is energy, vibrating at different frequencies and that all this energy transcends one state of existence to another. To start us out, here is my 21st century redefinition of energy:

> ***Energy is the primal, primary intelligent vibrating force or essence of all things in all states of existence - Quantum, Spiritual, and Physical***

Well and good, but what does this have to do with human consciousness and collective consciousness and the balance of energy? *The answer: all of existence is consciousness – part of the God Consciousness System - It is all energy and it is all connected, but, the world energy system – human/material consciousness - is out of balance.*

Let us look at the big picture for understanding. The truth is that the universe is God … is Pure Energy … is Pure Love, which is Pure Consciousness … which is the essence of all things within it. You, I, the earth, the galaxy, the solar system – birds, plants, mountains – all that you can see or perceive, it is all part of the God Consciousness system that permeates all life in the time/space continuum. It is all energy. So just for this moment, stop, pause, and become aware that you and I are manifestations of God. We are part of the consciousness system. We are God expressing as us. Once you become aware of this, you will never be the same. This is somewhat theological stuff, so we will not get into the detail of it here. But what we do need to talk about in detail is the human collective consciousness. This is where we need to develop the case for a *"A Tectonic Shift in Human Consciousness"*. Let us discover.

The perfection and Balance of Universal Energy is transcendent, so there is perfection in the natural order of things on the physical plane. Some call this Divine Order. However, we are dealing with humans and the energy of individual and collective human consciousness. Although the core of this energy is spiritual in nature, our decision energy the way we think, our choices and actions are often diametrically opposed to the spiritual energy of the Universe. Let me explain. Are we making choices and acting out of love, compassion, caring, and empathy, or, making choices out of hatred, fear, and divisiveness? Here is the thing. Our decision energy, which is consciousness, is either positive or negative (or neutral). Now, If our thought and decision process is negative, that energy goes out into the collective consciousness (energy) and draws this energy away from the natural order of spiritual consciousness. This causes and imbalance in the natural order of things. Now, if our thought and decision process is positive and uplifting, this energy goes out into the collective consciousness, which is energy and is pulled to or attracted to the natural order of spiritual consciousness, creating balance in the natural order of things. So here is the deal. For the last several thousands of years, our thinking, choices, and actions have been imbalanced to the negative creating a collective consciousness that is a dark cloud of negativity affecting the way we live. Is there some positiveness in this consciousness? Yes, but there has been a dramatic increase in the negative over the last 100 + years that is skewing the balance of the energy consciousness to the negative side … away from the spiritual order of things. Can we ever get back to a balance of energy forces in the world? Absolutely! … with a radical shift in world consciousness brought about by a dramatic increase in the expression of the Divine Feminine.

Individual Human Consciousness and The Collective Consciousness

What most of us know and accept is that consciousness is a function of the brain, which is the servomechanism of the human condition that provides a quality of awareness, the ability to experience or feel, or the executive control system of the mind. Keep in mind that we still do not know exactly what it is but let us start with that.

On the human plane, your mind/brain houses your consciousness. It is your storage POD for your consciousness – a digitized book - which is stuffed full of every thought, word, deed, and experience since day one on this planet. It is your life story, the script by which you conduct your life. Your consciousness is sometimes called you belief system, the lens of perception on how you see your world. It becomes the force behind the way you act and behave.

To make human mind/consciousness more understandable, let us use a computer analogy: The computer has a hard drive, a servomechanism just like the brain. Our brain/consciousness works like the computer. Our brain is the hard drive, the servomechanism. Our consciousness then, is the software added to the hard drive and includes everything we have experienced - like programming of sorts including specific software such as education and religion. It becomes the identity of the servomechanism. Everything we have experienced since day one until now is there ~ZAP, on the hard drive of our mind/brain. We have all heard of the terms inputs and outputs, garbage in-garbage out, and storage. It is pretty much the same concept. It becomes your personal POD of consciousness.

Very simply, we are the sum product of our life experiences. Each moment of our lives we are bombarded by literally thousands of stimuli, impulses, forces, and data external from us

...everything from people, things, conditions, and circumstances. All this "stuff" becomes the "programming" of our computer-like mind and becomes our consciousness, our personal identity. The startling thing to open your eyes to is that reportedly 85% plus of the programming is negative. For example, the average third grader watches over 1300hours of TV per year, watches the equivalent of 30 hours "R" rated programming, but only attends school for 800 hours per year. And what do you think is the association between the current video games sold to youth today and aggressive/violent behavior ...like road rage? What do you feed your mind before going to bed? The 11:00 news? And what is typically on the 11:00 news? It is all something to think about since all this becomes your operating consciousness. Although your experiences are being recorded, it is **YOUR THOUGHTS ABOUT IT** that make it personal to you. Our experiences build one on the other and our consciousness is continually expanding, growing, and unfolding and being shaped ...knowingly or unknowingly, and become our default behavioral mechanism for action.

So, who we are – our human consciousness, our digital brain book - is built one brick at a time over an extended period of time as we travel some rough as well as smooth roads. It is an overly complex issue and process. In addition to the complexity, there is also widespread belief that 99% of what and who we are cannot be touched or smelled and is invisible and intangible.

Pause for a moment and allow the complexity and awesomeness of your outer sphere of influence sink into your consciousness. Think about the who, what, where, when and why of the influences on your life from birth to now. Open your eyes and recognize that most of your early life consists of being programmed and brainwashed by "others" ...parents, teachers, coaches, other siblings (birth order), friends, neighbors, religious figures, etc. Think about what you know and why you know it. Some of my most meaningful growth experiences have come while exploring my beliefs and where they come from ...especially in the arena of religion. When I uncover false beliefs, I am better able to change or let them go. What I am saying is that we have been programmed ... and often by default, use this programming as a convenient excuse for non-performance; ...you made me do it ...I can't ...you didn't give me the tools ...it can't be done ...don't waste your time ...I don't have enough education ...I am too young/old ...not smart enough. Phycologists tell that by age 21, we are literally programmed with as many as three trillion messages and 500 mini concepts ...all of which becomes our mindset, our brain consciousness. Imagine at age 60 + the kind of programming we have undergone.

Stop for a moment and be aware, realize some of your programming, your consciousness, is positive and supportive in what you do. Too much of it is negative and becomes our nemesis that turns to self-criticism and doubt that stands in the way of us becoming all we can be. They become the negative emotions that have been stored up in the subconscious mind that we do not even realize are there. They tend to sabotage us. For example, often our behavior is the result of learned family habits and patterns such as anger, eating, and the need to be right. Here is the thing we all need to realize. It is called the Paradigm Rule.

The Paradigm Rule

Whatever your personal program, paradigm or belief system is at this moment, it controls and regulates all your actions, feelings, behavior, and abilities. Performance cannot go beyond the limits that you unconsciously placed upon yourself. Your inner belief system is so powerful and profound that you literally

cannot act inconsistently with it. Not only that, but pressure to go beyond your mental paradigm causes discomfort and disorientation. You are locked into, so to speak, the comfort zone you have created. You strongly resist any attempts to make you act in a way that is inconsistent with this incredibly strong inner belief system. Personal growth and change can be accomplished but must begin by increasing your mental paradigm ...expanding your mind/consciousness. This is usually done in small increments but
can be done in a quantum leap when accompanied by a significant emotional experience. As you expand your belief system - this is called a paradigm shift - your actions, feelings, behavior, and abilities automatically expand to fil it.

This my friend is the nature of your individual human/brain consciousness. As the Talmud states, "we don't see things as they are, we see them as we are." Now, add your POD of consciousness to the 7.5 billion other PODs of consciousness living in the world today, and then add all the other accumulative PODs of consciousness that have contributed to the world consciousness system over thousands and thousands of years, and you have what is called the Human Collective Consciousness in the time, space, matter plane of existence. It is an energy field of consciousness and It is all "recorded" and has both positive and negative impact on the current world situation.

To be more specific, the Human Collective Consciousness is what Jung referred to as the collective unconsciousness. Earnest Holmes, author of The Science of mind, described it as *"the sum of all the thoughts and actions of the ages, operating on a psychic level and psychic field that impinges on everyone"*. It is an existing energy field of thought accumulated since time immortal - energy that just is, that cannot be destroyed, but can and does change form. Can we access that information? The answer is yes, and we are just beginning to understand how. If you want an interesting read, check out the works and writings of psychic Edgar Casey who in the mid nineteen hundreds healed and assisted thousands by tapping into what he called the Akashic Records. He described the Akashic Records as a compendium of all human events, thoughts, words, emotions, and intent ever to have occurred in the past, present, or future. In a trance state, he was able to access the information he needed from the records and bring it back to the present and provide healing and solutions to people's personal problems. Think of the possibilities.

Here is the thing. It becomes a little frightening to realize that there are about 7.7 billion PODs of human consciousness in the world today. All these multibillion "different" individual PODs of consciousness have been running around, interconnected, bumping into each other - like the action of a pin ball machine - acting, overreacting, changing, growing, and linking up. These separate individual consciousness PODs, with different belief systems and paradigms, have been programmed to think that they are the only ones in touch with reality, when in fact, we are all living in our own world of illusions - an alternate reality, each different from the other based on how each was programmed. These programs are given to us from the illusions and programming from family, friends, religion, education, parents, teachers, and so on. Thus, we are all living our own illusion, and only a few have come even close to "seeing" reality. Jesus is one of those. What we see, and experience is just a very tiny piece of the most spectacular, deeper, and greater reality available to us on an elevated plane of consciousness, like Jesus. We will talk more about this when we talk about the tectonic shift needed in human consciousness.

So, the sad news is that we are steeped in a limited consciousness of some sort which is multilayered and deeply programmed. For most of us this is a world of illusions and fantasy. For some, a nightmare that we need awakened from. Some would say the consciousness we live in are thoughts and beliefs based on lies. It is NOT reality. It is not about the hard drive we have been given, but the consciousness we have been programmed with. The good news is that we can program/reprogram our human consciousness to better serve us. Part of that is to reawaken to the power of the spiritual realm, which we will get into later.

So, let us get back to the subject at hand – dethroning the systemic patriarchal social system. Based on what we have talked about and reviewed relative to consciousness and the collective consciousness, the "system" was developed over hundreds of years thought by thought, belief by belief, action by action that it has become systemic. We have been this way for so long, we have thought this way for so long, that we have accepted and normalized the resulting behavior as "just the way it is". We have all been programmed big time. We may not have liked it but allowed the "again cycle" to continue without major upheaval. Yes there were demonstrations and protests but major changes to the "system" did not occur. And then 2020 came and the perfect storm hit – the universe responded with an energy self-correcting initiative. This has brought about an awakening and critical mass has been reached. We the people will no longer accept the tyranny of the systemic patriarchs. "Enough", "Me Too", "Black lives Matter", "Save the Environment", "People not Profits", "love Over Hate", "Social Minded Leadership", and "Respect, Dignity, and Equal Rights for All Humanity". Life right now may seem like total chaos, but what we are experiencing are the symptoms of a spiritual emergence or and awakening to the positive transformation taking place in our world energy system. The old saying is true. Out of chaos comes order. Realize we are in the difficult stage of the transition from a primitive to an enlightened society. We are changing the collective consciousness one thought, belief, and action at a time. Pause for a moment and "see" the vision for a bright future.

"We are the Universe becoming conscious of itself"
Physicist John Wheeler

Next up we will be talking about the *state of the collective consciousness system*. We know it is not all that great, but there are some bright spots. The key is to always remember we are the ones that caused this collective consciousness by our thinking – which drives our behavior and actions and the resulting consequences. Here are a few things Albert Einstein said that applies to the conundrum we are in:

"The world as we have created it is a process of our thinking. It cannot be changed without changing our thinking."

"We cannot solve our problems with the same thinking we used when we created them. Insanity: doing the same thing over and over again and expecting different results. The measure of intelligence is the ability to change."

The State of the Collective Consciousness System

The world is rampant with deafening noise and chatter - 85% negative - all going into the human collective consciousness system. Today's chatter is cumulatively added to an already cloudy, murky mass that has evolved over millennia. If you took a picture today of the collective consciousness of the world you would see what someone from another visiting galaxy would see and sense as we presented in the Preface of this book and repeated here:

> *"The earth is a troubled world. There is overwhelming consciousness of negativity existing in earthlings. There is much hatred, violence, and separateness; many of its peoples live in poverty; famine and disease,*
> *many with health issues, while others live in opulence.*
>
> *Their airways are filled with negative vibrations coming from human thoughts and beliefs, violent and destructive programming from TV's, radio, and video gaming depicting hate, violence, separation, bias, and bigotry. They are obsessed 24/7 with mass digital pollution.*
>
> *They know not of their oneness. Racial bias, antisemitism, ethnic and cultural bias, bigotry, and gender inequity separate them and keep them from living the peace that is available to them. They live in ignorance of the spiritual realm and thus know not who they are: spiritual beings that have chosen to have a human experience on their planet.*
>
> *Crazy things are happening in their environment. The environment is screaming. The system is way out of balance with floods, fires, water quality and dirty air putting the planet and population in jeopardy. Animals, vegetation, and air quality are suffering immensely. They fail to see the interconnectedness of all things.*
>
> *One of the human population areas called The United States is in the process of an election of a leader they call President. There is no spiritual focus in the process and the earthlings are bound up in hate, divisiveness, and separation. Big government, big business,*

big pharmacy are forcing more separatism, while the suffering of individual humans is increasing.

Practice of White Nationalism, White Supremacy, racism, ethnic cleansing, antisemitism, racial profiling, – bigotry of all kinds, is keeping them in bondage, and they seem ignorant and unaware of how this is affecting the world consciousness and thus their lives.

Their world is polarized and separated in mind and spirit. Hawkish waring nations are posing nuclear threats on each other; they are in the midst of economic globalization but are hindered by cultural bias, trade wars, social and economic posturing, and wars. There are some good things going on, but the negative consciousness persists and is growing.

They are ignorant or unaware of who they truly are and the power of their being, and fail to see the world as a sacred, living, breathing organism with the interconnection of all things.

What this is saying is that the energy system of world is a little wonky – meaning the Yin and the Yang of this planet is so skewed the energy system is being forced into a self-correction process to avoid possible mass extinction. And since we do not want that to happen, it must be our choice to do what is necessary to rebalance the system. Let us take a look at just some of the specific things we humans have done in just the last several hundred years that have caused one of the biggest growing pains in the planets history and a negative dark night to the collective consciousness energy system. We will be presenting, outlining and reviewing several sub-energy systems in the world consciousness system so we can "see" what is causing the imbalance we are consciously and unconsciously sensing - to shine a light on the areas that caused the problem in the first place, and need our action and behavioral changes to avoid disaster. The areas we will be looking at include **the environment, world conflicts – wars, systemic misogyny, systemic racism including ethnic based discrimination, socioeconomic disparity, and viruses and plagues.** I refer to each of these as energy systems in their own right. All of these play a pivotal role in the balance of the world energy system and directly impact the collective consciousness system. So what this is about is the earth and its people experiencing major disturbances at their core, with the system rebelling. Pause and listen. You can see, perceive, and feel the tension. The world and our human/collective consciousness is in an epic crisis. The energy of the world is so critically unbalanced we are experiencing the consciousness system delivering a major self-correcting storm.

Consciously reviewing the energy surrounding each of these systems will open our eyes and make us aware of the massive energy imbalance existing in the world and sets us up for our case presentation of the need for **A Seismic Shift in Human Consciousness** and **The Rise of The Divine Feminine** as the energy of choice for change. We will conclude by offering some specific recommendations as to what needs to be done to restore the energy balance. Let us begin to "see"!

Energy Disturbances Affecting the Collective Consciousness

The Environment – an Ecological Disaster

It is time humankind fully realize the environment has a consciousness. Look around you. Everything you can see or touch. trees, animals, grass, mountains, streams, oceans, rocks …it is all energy and is part of and one with God Essence and it can be "hurt". We all have an enormous impact on this consciousness and have a responsibility to coexist in a complementary way. I became acutely aware of the "vibration" of nature and the environment during a week adventure in the Rocky Mountains.   That week became my "stop and smell the roses" exercise. I experienced a deep AWARENESS of the flow and oneness …the consciousness in nature. It all melds together …the mountains, snow, streams, rivers, air, wind, meadows, forest/trees, vegetation, animals, sky, clouds, rain, insects, and more. It is all One eco system …it is all energy …it has a consciousness and I became AWARE of being an integral part of it. Do you know we can talk to trees, birds, animals - the environment? By "talking" I mean sensing and relating to the "vibrations" of all that surrounds us.

Nature has much to share with us. When we listen closely, we can hear her speak - "Help! I am being suffocated, I can't breathe, stop what you are doing, please, be loving and compassionate toward me, be environmentally responsible; it hurts me when you don't". We are experiencing **Environmental degradation at its worst – Ouch!**

The environment is screaming. The system is way out of balance with floods, fires, water quality and dirty air putting the planet and population in jeopardy. Animals, vegetation, and air quality are suffering immensely. We see the symptoms – climate change, increasing floods, fires, dirty air, polluted water, melting ice sheets, warmer oceans and more. Now remember it is all energy and it is all connected, but it is being changed -in form – to a negative unbalanced energy. This is not good for the planet and all its inhabitants. What is causing this? Most of us know the reasons but let us give some specific details.

Study after study show that humans are to blame for the negative shift in the energy environment of the planet – all driven by population growth. With disregard to the climate, we have demanded "more" of everything. More manufacturing of goods and services - housing, automobiles, appliances, and toys of all sorts. To do this we have had to gear up production using enormous amounts of fossil fuels – gas, oil, coal that produce a corresponding amount of carbon dioxide pollution, a greenhouse gas that is released into the atmosphere. It is called greenhouse gas because it produces a greenhouse effect, or a warmer environment like in a greenhouse. So, the carbon pollution is trapped in our atmosphere making the earth warmer and dirtier, resulting in often radical shifts and changes in climate. A significant amount of this heat ends up in our oceans causing melting ice sheets and wild shifts in climate. Human caused global warming is a fact.

In addition, the population explosion came with advances in modes of transportation that has resulted in production of hundreds of millions of trucks and automobiles. The combustion process in the engines that fuel these transports produce massive amounts of carbon dioxide and carbon monoxide, adding to the warmer dirtier air. To round out our air pollution woes, add the Methane and Nitrous oxide emissions from agriculture and non-environmentally safe products (aerosols, etc.). Another significant impact on air quality is deforestation. Building more homes, factories, and businesses requires clearing land – deforestation. When this happens, a substantial portion of the "forest" – trees and vegetation that eat carbon and produce oxygen have been wiped out, and oxygen/carbon balance in our atmosphere has been critically impacted. Mass destruction of rain forests in Central and South America, Africa, and Southeast Asia have been particularly devastating to the climate cause.

Another key factor in the degradation of the environment is human waste. More humans means more waste. Overflowing landfills, randomly discarded plastics and other non-biodegradable materials in oceans, rivers, and streams virtually everywhere are killing us and killing wildlife. And do not forget about Industry dumping manufacturing waste products and chemicals that pollute our ground water. And then we have agriculture using poisonous chemicals that infiltrate our food and water supply.

Let us talk about the food supply. In 1913 agricultural crops were 100% farmer owned and were 100% non-GMO. In 2013, agricultural crops were 95% corporate owned and 90% GMO. In addition, much of our food we eat today are processed conglomerates with added chemicals, starches, and sugars. This is a major cause of the energy in our human body being out of alignment - out of sync. When this happens, our immune systems are compromised and we as a society are more receptible to disease and sickness, like colds and viruses.

And we would be remiss if we did not mention there are several natural factors responsible for climate change including continental drift, volcanoes, ocean currents, the earth's tilt, comets, and meteorites. That got me thinking universally about our environment and things like global warming. Part of the change in our environment is cyclical and we have no control over that ...but we are a BIG part of the negative change in the environment because of the decisions and choices we are making and have made.

We have been hearing scientists say that if we do not take action to correct the climate disaster we have caused, then we are in deep trouble. The environment is self-correcting, and we will all pay a huge price if we do not respond. The good news is human-caused climate change can be human-solved climate change. You can "see" from the above, there is a high degree of urgency to act. My conclusion is that we all are in integral part of the stream of Pure Consciousness which includes nature. It is time to step up and be responsible.

Distressed Consciousness From World Conflicts and Wars

There is and has been a devastating effect on the world energy system due to world conflicts and wars. Let us open our eyes and be aware of what we have done to the world and ourselves.

> **WWI** had a devastating impact on the world energy system. According to Wikipedia, there were an estimated 40 million deaths, and although this might sound high, the numbers included military and civilians. The civilian count included those in the way of conflict along with war related hunger, famine, disease, and war crimes. Add to this the long-term suffering of the wounded and the financial and economic impact on the world population. That is a lot of negative energy put into the system.

> **WWII** was the deadliest conflict in history. According to Wikipedia, 70-85 million people perished due to causes mentioned under WWI. Tragic, and for what. **The negative vibrations coming from any conflict often originate from feelings about culture differences and religion, and, unforgiveness (I was wronged). These originate from heavy dense energy like fear, anger, resentment, hate, greed (territory), and the need for dominance and power**. As you think about it you can feel the negativity in warring conflicts.

What we will see as we go through the state of the world and the energy imbalance situations is that most of the negative consciousness we experience today is deeply rooted – developed over eons of time, allowed to fester and now unconscious and part of an overwhelming negative and systemic normality. Once you are aware of this, you instinctively know what to do to change it. The key to change is awareness and the willingness to bring the system back to balance.

> **Other notable warring conflicts** the USA has been involved in the last one hundred years include Korea, Vietnam, Iraq, and Afghanistan. Although casualties were less than the world wars, significant costs have been are being paid by many nations and their people. Hunger, despair, poverty, loss of limbs, homes and life, PTSD, and suicides to name a few. Try to feel the stress and strain on the energy system – our collective consciousness, and always ask the question, why? Is it not about time for a seismic shift in consciousness?

Up front we postulated that the systemic patriarchal monarchy type social system was the cause of the "perfect storm" we are experiencing. When it comes to conflicts and wars, who in a social system makes the decisions, and for what reasons. Remember what the aliens say:

> *Their world is polarized and separated in mind and spirit. Hawkish waring nations are posing nuclear threats on each other; they are in the midst of economic globalization but are hindered by cultural bias, trade wars, social and economic posturing, and wars. There are some good things going on, but the negative consciousness persists and is growing.*
>
> *They are ignorant or unaware of who they truly are and the power of their being, and fail to see the world as a sacred, living, breathing organism with the interconnection of all things.*

Yes, it is time to dethrone the systemic patriarchal system and make the full transition to an enlightened society with a new dawn for the environment and human rights.

Systemic Misogyny

What exactly is Misogyny? According to Wikipedia, misogyny is:
> ... the hatred of, contempt for, or prejudice against women or girls. Misogyny manifests in numerous ways, including social exclusion, sex discrimination, hostility, patriarchy, male privilege, belittling of women, disenfranchisement of women, violence against women, and sexual objectification.

This segment of the world's energy imbalance in the collective conscious is broad-based but is generally centered around women's rights. Specific rights include the right to bodily integrity and autonomy, to be free from sexual **violence**, to have equal rights under the law, fair wages - or equal pay, and to have reproductive rights, and be elevated to positions of power. For thousands of years an ingrained cultural structure in our patriarchal society has consciously and unconsciously perpetuated the massive systemic power imbalances we are experiencing today. For all these years, women have been incumbered with imposed male dominance, implied superiority, and sexual abuse leading to the sexism, racism and economic inequities experienced today. We are beginning to wake up, and a big part of that awakening is being initiated by women.

For women, the struggle for equal rights has been going on for centuries. Women have been seeking economic and political equality along with social reforms for centuries. It has been a struggle all the way. It was not until the mid-19th century when women's rights took a positive turn when the women's suffrage movement became heated and active – initiated primarily by women that formed national and international women's organizations to coordinate efforts. In addition to the right to vote, this movement included broad-based equal rights for women.

For women in the United States, the ingrained systemic abuse of women's rights is centuries old and was passed down from European male monarchs through the immigration process. The culture brought by the immigrants to the United States included social and political systems where only male citizens who owned land were permitted to vote and who ultimately were given or assumed the power and authority over the laws and rules of society. This was the beginning of the systemic patriarchal system. Think about the ongoing battle that took place – from the mid 1800's – until on June 4, 1919 when congress passed, and then ratified on August 18, 1920, the 19th amendment granting women the right to vote. Think about this for a moment. The initial development of the earth started 4 billion years ago, and it took almost all that time before women had the right to vote. And now in 2020 the fierce struggle continues. It is hard to believe it took all this time for the imbalance in feminine and masculine energy to finally reach a state of thoughtful consideration.

An important wave in the women's movement is the one against sexual harassment and sexual assault. Women have become increasingly vocal about the patriarchal dominant culture dealing with sexism and 2006 the phrase "Me Too" was initially used in social media to target behavioral patterns dealing with sexual harassment and sexual assault. In 2017, widespread media coverage of sexual assault allegations against Harvey Weinstein opened the floodgates of women banning together and the "Me Too" movement went viral on sexual abuse, sexual harassment, and domestic violence against women.

The latest blatant example of systemic misogynist behavior came on July 21,2020 when U.S. Representative Ted Yoho allegedly shouted out a profane slur at Rep Alexandria Ocasio-

Cortez on the Capital steps after a policy disagreement. This is just one of many offensive name calling incidents attributable to a systemic patriarchal behaviors trying to quiet women and put them on the defensive. The good ole boy network had always been successful in forcing a "stay in your place" regimen. But not this time. This time Cortez called out Yoho in a powerful speech against misogyny in Congress. It is on the record and it is about time. This is an incredibly positive sign for a shift in consciousness and the transformation to an enlightened society. Here is the thing though. There are hundreds of systemic patriarchal monarchy types in Congress that have a misogynistic penchant. This includes Trump, McConnell, Barr, and all their enablers in both the House and Senate whether Republican or Democrat. They all need to be retired. There is a toxic masculinity that exists in Congress and across the world. It is systemic and needs called out and eradicated.

The "Me Too" movement has gone a long way to remove the societal blinders and given all a sense of the magnitude of the problem. It has led to needed criticism, backlash, and firings across America. Silence has been broken but it is still not enough. Women are still anxious and cautious when going out alone to walk, jog, or bike. When we talk about racism, we will show a similar feeling from black men when they are out and about - but in their case it is about always looking over their shoulder in fear of racial injustice incidents.

Lack of Women in Positions of Power – Leadership and Decision Making

One of the struggles that underlies society is limited or often ineffective decision making in the corporate boardrooms, social justice systems, and in politics. It is time we wake up and "see" that 50% of the brains or talents in the world – women - are not represented in positions of power in our social structures.

Absent in the mix of critical decisions is socially conscious values and has led to discriminatory practices in all the arenas in society including education, equal pay, equal rights, sexism, humanitarian parity, access to equal opportunity, and imbalance of the world energy system. As Kamala Harris, Democratic U.S. senator from California has said,

"If you're trying to solve the world's problems, you should hear from half the world's population."

What we will be bringing to light in "The Rise of the Divine Feminine" is that women bring a more holistic and wholeistic perspective to decision making at the table. Following up on Kamala Harris's quote, the authors quote is:

"Women oftentimes make far superior and more effective decisions because they include more of societal values in the equation – like compassion, listening, empathy, and understanding. This is not a weak position as represented in a patriarchal view, but a demonstration of strength and understanding that makes decisions more effective for all"

If you understand that quote you will realize we could enhance effective decision making by far greater than 50%. That applies to all sectors of society including elevated levels of the corporate world. Now, that said, society is making minor progress, but There have been some recent encouraging moments. One of those moments was the 2016 run for President by a woman, Hillary Clinton. Although that was not successful, even though she won the popular vote, it showed the patriarchal system still entrenched.

Then we moved to another encouraging moment in the 2018 congressional elections when 100 women were sworn in to the 116 Congress, with many more running that did not make it. Even with this, the United States ranks #75 out of 193 countries in terms representation of women in government. Hope still rises, and in 2019 six women stepped up to bid for the

Democratic nominee for President in the 2020 Presidential election. That did not happen, but as of this writing, the presumptive nominee in the Democratic Party for President, Joe Biden, promised to have a woman as his VP running mate. With these significant gains, the patriarchal system is beginning to bend, and we should all look forward to the day, soon, where gender equality is not an issue in politics or any other segment of our society. So how do we get there?

Carl Jung said, *"until you make the unconscious conscious, it will direct your life, and you will call it fate."* In other words, you cannot change what you are not aware of. This goes back to the explanation how the proliferation of the patriarchal system happened – somewhat unconsciously, over centuries. If we can expose it and bring it to the light of day and consciously change the behavior, we can balance the world energy system. That means consciously taking steps to dethrone the patriarchal system, a system that consciously or unconsciously supports, fosters, imposes male dominance, implied superiority, and sexual abuse leading to the sexism, racism, and economic inequities over women that we have experienced for centuries. How do you overcome this seeming mountain? We are going to tackle this one step at a time through thought, word, action, and behavior change - women demanding action. We will discuss the "how" in more detail in the chapter "Decision 2020".

Here is what a patriarchal system looks like. Regardless of a woman's experience, education, race or ethnicity, or abilities, our societal cultural system fosters and promotes **untruths** - that women are less qualified and less competent than men; that a strong and intelligent women just upset and disrupt the natural order of our (male run) social systems; that women are too weak and emotional for rational decision making; are not worthy of the same opportunities as men; that women should always be subordinate to men in positions of power – men are more capable of handling tough situations; women are better off sticking with fashion and beauty, that is their strength. Here is an example of how a patriarchal system manifest itself in the past. When graduating from high school, my wife wanted to go to college to become a forest ranger. "the system" told her that "girls" only go to college to become social workers, nurses, or teachers. Hogwash! When it is all finished, **a true - balanced patriarch statement will read:**

> *"Women are just as competent, capable, worthy, mentally tough, and intelligent as men to occupy positions of power and make the strategic decisions to move us forward. This is to be a world of a balanced, shared, and respected female/male energy system. Women can be or do anything they want to be or do, and receive the same recognition, rewards, and benefits as men. From this day forward, the human energy system of the world will be a balance of male/female energy and that energy used in the most effective way. This is how we balance world energy"*

To help us visualize what a good balanced female/male energy system looks like, let me offer an example of the thriving marriage between two people. Firsts and foremost, the couple enter their marriage with a conscious commitment to see their relationship as partners, lovers, and helpmates – always having each other's back. Timely and key discussions and agreement will be had for major decisions in their lives – where to live, major purchases, family, pets, friends, entertainment, etc., discussing, and being aware of their input to the other. The key to success in an effective powerful marriage is communication ... listening, and understanding, then, developing a common goal or mission, then, developing a plan and jointly executing the plan to the best of their common ability. Realize that in this kind of relationship one plus one equals 3 or 4. There is tremendous power when two people come together with commitment, respect, and dignity to make themselves and the world better. It is even more powerful when women are in the mix.

Think of all the missed opportunities in business, industry, politics, religion - the lost energy and talents - when women are kept out of positions of power. When men and women come together, regardless of the situation, remarkable things happen. In the process of coming together, here are a few reminders:

- Start with an agreement on goals, expectations, mission, and intentions
- Focus on strengths and similarities, not weaknesses
- In terms of self, Know there is no one better than you and no one worse than you
- Allow disagreements but always negotiate the best possible solution for all concerned
- Compromise is always an option, not a failure
- A diverse team is always stronger
- Always have each other's back.
- Key to any relationship is communications – sharing, discussing, listening, understanding, and compromise – with mutual respect

Can you imagine the positive energy influx to the world energy system and the brightening of the collective consciousness when we finally eliminate systemic misogyny. To do this there is an extensive need to "vision it, see it, act with intention, organize, protest, sit-in, stand up, and vote. By doing so we will be creating and equalized balance of power!

BELIEVE AND ACT AS IF

Systemic Racism and Ethnic-based discrimination

Racism is a systemic plague woven into the collective consciousness fabric of the United States since early in our history. Be aware, racism has a gigantic negative impact on the collective consciousness of the planet. The big problem is that as a society we are not even conscious of the systemic inbreeding of racism and how it manifests itself in ugly, aggressive, threatening, dangerous, ill-tempered, and often violent unconscious behavior that permeates all aspects of life for all of society. Time to wake up and realize that racism is in the fabric of every individual - that means you, that means me. We need to open our eyes and "see" that racism is a thick dense negative energy that has a massive negative impact on the lives of all Americans. It needs to be addressed and eradicated. This negativity can be reversed, but as the old saying goes, *you cannot change what you do not "see".* So, let us just "SEE".

We know that racism has been inbred in the United States from the very start. In the period of the colonial era, white American men, predominately affluent white Anglo-Saxon protestants were given, or should we say assumed control of certain social and legal privileges and rights and denied or excluded the same rights and privileges to other races and minorities. These exclusions or limitations have been with us from day one in our history and continue to negatively impact all races and minorities in matters of wealth, education, immigration, voting rights, citizenship, land acquisition and criminal justice. This is not new; it has been happening for hundreds of years.

Early in our history key targets of ethnicity-based discrimination went to the Irish, Poles, and Italians – Non-Protestant immigrants. Here we are in the 21st Century and our American society continues to experience high intensities of racism and discrimination. The largest segment of society affected is the African Americans, but the list also includes Hispanic and Latino Americans, Arab Americans, and Jewish Americans. Racism is inbred in the American culture. It is systemic and has become so elusive and subtle that we are now blind to what this virus has and is doing to our society and world. When we begin to really "see" this we will realize the source is the systemic patriarchal social system instigated hundreds of years ago. We will deal with this in more detail shortly.

Native Americans:
One of the first peoples on the list of systemic racism is Native Americans. My heart aches to think what we did to these people. We seized their land, imprisoned, enslaved, and massacred them, then enclosed them on segregated reservations. They are one of the most deprived American peoples today struggling to exist. They have limited, often nonexistent utility infrastructure (water, sewer, electric, roads), dilapidated homes and housing, poor educational facilities and opportunity, nonexistent economic opportunity, poor, limited or no health care, live in a food desert, and have extremely limited social support. Our systemic patriarchal system is responsible for this. This is manifest racism at its worst! There is no excuse for how these people have been and are continually treated! Open your eyes America!

LGBTQ Community: finally on June 20, 2020 the Supreme Court extended the protections of Title VII of the Civil Rights Act of 1964 to LGBTQ community preventing discrimination in employment. This is just one small step in systemic discrimination. There is still more to be done in this arena for expanding the rights and privileges of the LGBTQ community. Stay tuned.

Slavery – African Americans – Black and Brown Systemic Racism:

Slavery turned racism. To me this is bigger than any plague from the very beginning of our history that is still playing itself out. Some have called this the original sin of our country. Racism is probably todays biggest unconscious systemic arena in our society. The ironic thing is we know it, but we do not know it. It has become so much a part of our culture that until recently we have not even been consciously aware of it. We now know that systemic racism is imbedded so deeply that a major undertaking is necessary to expose it, and another herculin effort needed to make it right.

Take your blinders off for a moment. Tell me you "see" what slavery did to these people. Put yourself in their shoes of the black man for a moment. Feel the degradation, the pain, the suffering. Tell me how you felt when your slave owner Thomas Jefferson announced he was launching a "scientific" inquiry to prove that you a black, were inferior to him and all whites. Can you see that from this point on, racial discrimination against you, a black, became a systemized social structure that has lasted hundreds of years and is reaching an intense crescendo here in 2020.

Even though President Lincoln was successful in getting the Emancipation Proclamation passed on January 1, 1863 that guaranteed freedom for blacks, it essentially did not take place until what we now celebrate as "Juneteenth" – June 19, 1865 when it was finally accepted in the South. We say that freedom came to the blacks in 1865 but in actuality we know that the systemic racist system was and continues to be so deeply ingrained in the United States that freedom has never totally happened. Freedom for black Americans is still illusive. As a nation we must come to the realization that we are not free until we are all free. The tragedy throughout US history is that African Americans have continually faced restrictions on their political, social, and economic freedoms. This racism continues today to manifest itself in socioeconomic inequality that limits black/brown opportunities in employment, housing, education, lending, and government. It is outright discrimination in the United States that permeates all aspects of life in all communities of color … and seriously impairs human society from becoming all that we can be. Stop and see it - a serious human rights struggle going on in the United States causing a major imbalance in the world energy system.

We speak of freedom, yet 56 years after Juneteenth, in 1921 the "Tulsa Massacre" took place where whites totally wiped out Greenwood, a community referred to as Black Wallstreet out of fear they were getting too powerful. This is as despicable as what we did to the Native Americans early in our history. How would you feel if you were one of the Greenwood citizens?

Again, put yourself into the shoes of an African American in his or her neighborhood. Feel your plight. You are now more susceptible to hunger, disease, low paying jobs, spotty health infrastructure, food deserts, degraded educational access and opportunity. Add to this, there are increasing cases of vigilante justice targeting blacks and browns including police brutality. You are always looking over your shoulder when you do the simplest of things like walking down the street. Time to wake up and really "see" the extent of the racist plague.

Yes, we have had some moments of awakening in our recent history triggered by brutal beatings, killings, and lynching of blacks by white supremacists and police - all an affront or insult to the dignity, respect, and rights of blacks. Over the last 100 years of our history there have been thousands of protests and racial riots, some of which were intense and brutal with loss of life and destruction of property. One of the key markers in recent history was the beginning of the civil rights movement and the 1968 assignation of Martin Luther King, Jr. In April and May of 1968, MLK's assassination triggered protests and riots in over 125 major cities in the US. There seemed to be an awakening, and there was to some extent, but the systemic racists culture smothered any real action for change, and complacency set in. It was just a part of the "again cycle", moments when events of incidents of racism occur, nothing happens, and the cycle continues to repeat itself. Protests and riots followed the beating of Rodney King, the Cincinnati riots in 2001, Police shooting of Oscar Grant in 2009, the shooting of Michael Brown in 2014, the death of Freddie Gray in 2015, the fatal shooting of Sylville Smith and Keith Lamont Scott by police in 2016. This is all part of the "again cycle" and we still are ignorant of the real cause, systemic racism, a product of the systemic patriarchal social system. The slogan "Black lives Matter" is a very appropriate. You cannot fix it if you do not know it. We are beginning to "see" it and act in a mighty way.

Perhaps the moment of awakening is now upon us. The death of George Floyd, an African American man occurred in Minneapolis on May 25, 2020 when a white police officer knelt on Floyd's neck for 8 minutes and 46 seconds and snuffed the life right out of George. For what? An alleged forgery charge. The incident was captured on video and subsequently viewed by millions. As of this writing, there has been racial riots and weeks of protests in over 125 cities - in all 50 states and in over 25 other countries. In the midst of the civil unrest there was an interesting Facebook posting that went something like this: *If you don't like a few days of protests and rioting you would really hate 400 years of systemic oppression and discrimination. Riots and protests are the language of the unheard.* "Black Lives Matter"

With this major civil unrest there is evidence that the "again cycle" may have been broken. The reason, THIS TIME IT IS DIFFERENT. A major difference is the diversity of the millions of protesters. Showing up to be counted are young and old - blacks, browns, whites, Asians, and Latinos - a rainbow of colors. Results of a survey showed that 87% of Americans feel there is systemic racism in the US, and the time for doing something about it is now. In addition, there is finally concerted movement by legislators at all levels for change in the justice system to include police reform. And finally, policy changes are needed to address systemic inequality in health care, education, and economic opportunity. In the end it is up to you and me.

The title of this book is "Dethroning the Systemic Patriarchal Social System". The premise here is when it comes to systemic racism, the law of cause and effect has been operational for hundreds of years and rooted in the systemic patriarchal social system. The dethroning has started and needs to continue with fever. We will get into the "how" in the "Decision 2020" chapter.

When it comes to handling systemic racism on the front lines, I would like to share some words of wisdom from the late civil rights icon, John Lewis, who passed on July 17, 2020. These words are very appropriate in today's age:

> *"… rioting, looting, and burning is not the way. Organize, demonstrate. Sit-in stand up. Vote. Be constructive, not destructive."*

> *"It doesn't matter when we are black or white or Latino, Asian American or Native American. It doesn't matter when we are straight or gay. We are one people, we are all one family, we all live in the same house. We must choose love over hate, courage over fear."*

Here are some powerful words from past President Barak Obama:

> *"… it falls on all of us … to work together to create a "new normal" in which the legacy of bigotry and unequal treatment no longer infects our institutions or our hearts."*

As a society we are becoming more conscious of racial bias. Independent research is now being done on police bias by studying individual incident reports on police action on similar "stops" of whites compared to blacks and Hispanics. The findings show African American and Hispanic individuals are treated more forcibly, searched more, and cuffed more than whites for a similar offense, and, blacks are 2.5 times more likely to be shot and killed. These studies confirmed that racial bias is not only widespread but after observing the reports and checking their own behavior, many police admitted not even being aware of their bias – that it is so systemic that it just happens. This is resulting in extensive reform in police funding, tactics, and training. The problem to date is that it is being done by 18,000 different law enforcement jurisdictions. With heightened emphasis on police bias there is now reform measures that will be dictated on a federal level with new laws, rules, and policies and will include a notional data base bringing higher transparency to law enforcement.

Here is the bottom line. Racism and ethnic based discrimination is causing a serious imbalance of energy in the consciousness system. What we are saying is that racism has a gigantic negative impact on the collective consciousness of the planet. Please recognize that racism is and has been systemic and unconscious since the beginning of our history. This plague has infected all the new tens of millions of our population since those early days. Racism has become a huge ball of negative energy existing in our collective consciousness system and a seismic shift is necessary to eradicate it from our culture. It needs addressed and a serious plan of implementation is needed.

For racial bias and discrimination, the tipping point has been reached. The systemic patriarchal system – especially as applies to racism and discrimination has been exposed, recognized, and is being dealt with. The new mantra in America is organize, demonstrate, sit-in, stand up, strategize, plot, plan, and vote. It may appear to be chaotic, but it is simply the universe making an automatic correction in balancing the energy of human consciousness. Be a maverick and do your part … and do it in a peaceful, non-violent, and spiritual way.

> *"I prayed for 20 years but received no answer until I prayed with my legs"*
>
> Frederick Douglas

> *"It is in your hands to create a better world for all who live in it"*
>
> Nelson Mandela

Black Lives Matter

Dethrone the Systemic Patriarchal Social System

Socioeconomic Disparity

Today, socioeconomic disparity is causing a gigantic inferno in the world energy system and a thickening of the dark murky fog in the collective consciousness. For us humans it is pushing us one step closer to the cliff. What is going on? Let us start at the beginning.

We have seen that our country was born with a systemic patriarchal system that continues today. This system dictates a socioeconomic structure that perpetrates inequities and access to resources due to limited opportunities in education, income, and employment. This systemic problem has its roots in a patriarchal system that controls with privilege, power, and control. The system has existed from the inception of our country, but over the last century we have seen a pronounced widening in the gap in socioeconomic status between the "haves" and "have nots". As a result of this disparity many "have nots" are now living in absolute poverty which is adversely affecting their health and lifestyles. Low-socioeconomic status households have less income or wealth to buffer against adverse events in life, especially their health. We are seeing some of this being played out in the women's movement, in civil unrest with protests and demonstrations against racism, and the current Corona Virus pandemic. Seemingly, the system continues to worsen. What is causing this? Why is there so much poverty in the United States and the world when the world has all the resources it will ever need at our disposal? The answer, the system is unbalanced, driven by the systemic patriarchal system and capitalism which is the economic subsystem. What we are "seeing" and experiencing is exactly how the system was built.

There is still such a thing as the American dream, but it is only accessible to those connected to the system and to a few who achieve the dream as a spin-off from the system culture and are "allowed" to prosper. Because of sexism, racism, and poverty, many are "systematically" deprived of a dream opportunity. The ugly part of the systemic patriarchal system is that it created a lot of wealth and prosperity for the "privileged" class at the expense of the "have nots". What we have pushed into the background and silenced for hundreds of years is that the wealth and prosperity of this great nation was and still is built on the backs of the slaves – African Americans, poor whites, Latinos, Mexicans, Asians, and other immigrants. But the rich keep getting richer and the poor keep getting poorer. This type of wealth building has been going on for years. It is systemic, and it is still controlled by the patriarchal system. Think about it. Whoever sets the rules and policy and writes the laws controls the outcome. Who is doing that today? Up to this point mostly elderly white males in government and industry. And, what is the profile of the pre- 2016 US Congress? But going back to 2014, I remember then President Barack Obama speaking out about the GOP's willingness "to say no to everything." He was speaking out about the Senates obstructionist tactics against his administration trying to do everything they could to defeat democratic ideals. He gave some important clues that highlighted the systemic patriarchal system we face today. Here is what he said: "Their willingness to say no to everything – the fact that since 2007, they have filibustered about 500 pieces of legislation that would help the middle class just gives you a sense of how opposed they are to any progress – has actually led to an increase in cynicism and discouragement among the people who were counting on us to fight for them. The conclusion is, well, nothing works … and the problem is, is that the folks worth fighting for - the person who is cleaning up that house or hotel, for the guy who used to work on construction but now has been laid off – they need us. Not because they want a handout, but because they know that government can serve and important function in unleashing the power of our private sector."

Now I realize that politics plays a significant role in what happens in our world, but during the economic recession which hit in 2007 -2008, I had a major epiphany. First, I lost my small business to the recession, and second, I had an awakening – I began to "see" with clarity that the gamesmanship of the systemic patriarchal system is preventing us from being all that we could be. The "system" is an obstructionist system catering only to those values that keep it in power. That is the time when I shifted my political mindset and registration from Republican to Democrat … but then and always, think and vote Independent as to what best serves humankind. My awareness has peaked since the 2016 election as I watch the heightened ugliness of the systemic patriarchal system manifest itself in the policies, decisions, and actions of the current White House Administration and the patriarchal enablers in the Congress that supports systemic control. It is a pathetic narcissistic attempt to maintain the "system at all costs". This has totally stifled the energies of our society.

We all need to take a good look, become aware of, and "see" what is causing the wide gaps and disparity in the socioeconomic energy system of the US and the world. If we cannot see it, we will never be able to address it and fix it. If we want to live in paradise, it is up to each one of us create it.

It is becoming clear that sexism, racism, and poverty - independently and together – are the systemic plagues driving the disparity in the socioeconomic system. Here is some supporting information to ponder.

- The wealthiest 1% of families in the US hold about 40% of all wealth
- The bottom 90% of families in the US hold less than one-quarter of all wealth; 25% of families have less than $10,000 in wealth

- According to the Census Bureau, in 2018, households in the top fifth of earners, with incomes of $130,000 or more brought in 52% of all US income. This is more than the lower four-fifths combined.
- 63% of Latino, 54% of blacks, 40% Asian American, and 37% of white workers earn less than poverty level income. (Metropolitan Policy Program at Bookings)
- Inequitable distribution of wealth is causing widespread poverty, hunger, homelessness, illiteracy, polluted air, and water
- There is limited access to equal opportunity for poor Latinos, blacks, and whites
- Projected military spending (October 1, 2020 through September 30, 2021) is $934 billion. After Social Security it is the second largest item in the budget
- Today, a woman earns 80 cents for every dollar a man earns. The pay gap is considerably more for black and Latino women.
- Cost of childcare is now more expensive than in-state college tuition making it difficult to go to work or get an advanced education.
- Reproductive rights have been under relentless attack at a time when access to safe abortion services is critical to the health and economic future of millions of women
- More women go to college than men but unequal pay burdens financial recovery
- More women are minimum wage workers than men, but minimum wage no longer keeps a mom and her baby out of poverty.

Because of the disparity in the socioeconomic system there has been a horrific denial of dignity to low income people generation after generation. Those on the wrong end of the stick have limited potential for a good education, employment, and wealth building. Ultimately, they feel less of themselves and end up taking the low paying jobs, often less than minimum wage, and are predisposed to poverty. These are gross inequities in the socioeconomic arena.

The systemic patriarchal system is designed to keep "those people" in their places. Wealth continues to grow for the wealthy and it is being done on the backs of the poor blacks and whites and non-privileged immigrants. Who would ever be so bold to reduce Social Security, Medicare and Medicaid and eliminate all other poverty initiatives. The same people giving the breaks to the rich. So, it is time to really look at the ugly side of the systemic patriarchal system and learn the truth about racism, oppression, segregation, lack and denial of dignity. Take a good look at who is making the laws, rules, policies that continue to support this ugly system. We can no longer just "talk about" policy, laws, rules, and changes. We need to change the people, starting with our Congress – especially the Senate leaders and those who have enabled the current administration by continually manipulating and supporting the old systemic patriarchal system.

But, when we become aware of the problem, some of the solutions seem obvious. Increase the minimum wage, develop solid anti-racism policies and laws, expand the Earned Income Tax to low income families, give more tax breaks to low income, invest in free education at all levels, pay for child care for low income families, end residential segregation, shift federal assets from the military to eliminate poverty, push for a socially conscious capitalistic structure where the rich owners and industry pay their fair share of taxes to lift the economy, and mostly, change the people that are making the rules and laws that support the pro systemic patriarchal system.

So, let me ask a pointed question. Is our systemic patriarchal system making America great (again)? Hopefully, you can see we are not so great now, BUT we can be great amongst the greatest. It will take a seismic paradigm shift in our consciousness – the way we think, behave, and act. It is time to leave behind the primitive illusion we have been living under and move on to a new paradigm of an enlightened society with a spiritual mindset. It is a mindset of love and compassion where we know we are equal, treated equal and have equal opportunity to life, liberty, and the pursuit of happiness. We are all brothers and sisters of the ONE. It makes no difference whether you are young, old, black, white, yellow, red, men, women, gay, or straight.

Okay, now to the tough discussion. We need to switch gears now and talk about Capitalism, another major reason for the disparity in the socioeconomic system. According to Wikipedia, Capitalism is an economic system based on the private ownership of the means of production and their operation for profit. Characteristics central to capitalism include private property, capital accumulation, wage labor, and voluntary exchange. In a capitalist market economy, decision-making and investments are determined by every owner of wealth, property, or production ability in financial and capital markets.

Look at these terms to describe capitalism; "private ownership", "private property", "capital accumulation", "wage labor", and "decisions made by every owner of wealth, property, or production ability". Wow, this automatically excludes a sizable portion of individuals in the US, and the world. Then add to this the fact that the rules, laws, and policies governing wealth are made by a systemic patriarchal system and you have a recipe for disaster. This disaster continues to exacerbate an already unbalanced socioeconomic system.

What we do not realize is that we are in the third phase of the evolution of the world social system. Here is an insight I learned from Mike Dooley who produces and sends out five days a week "Notes from the Universe". This is the one from June 2, 2020:

> *Primitive societies live by the Rule of might, and the strong prevail*
>
> *Advanced societies live by the Rule of law, and the privileged prevail*
>
> *Enlightened societies live by the Rule of love, and everyone is lifted higher*
>
> The Universe

As pointed out by Mike Dooley in Notes From the Universe, we have progressed from a **primitive society** and lived by the rule of might where the strong prevailed. Then we moved on to a more **advanced society** where we lived by the rule of law and the privileged prevailed with capitalism as the economic system. The third phase we are moving into is the **enlightened society** phase where we are to live by the rule of love where everyone is a contributor and shares in the wealth system. It will be difficult for pure capitalism to be the economic system of choice. So, before we completely implode, we need to decide what kind of economic system to put in place for our coming enlightened society.

Realize that capitalism is a large part of the systemic problem and it will be difficult moving into the "enlightenment" phase without a major change. Let me explain with one simple example. As seen and shared on Facebook is this eye opening truth: *"It is wild how so many Americans view the outsourcing of domestic manufacturing to China over the past 25 years as some devious Chinese plan for domination rather than a strategy by which the American ruling class exploded its profit margin by exploiting global inequity."* Ask yourself some questions. Where are these profits going? Who is really benefiting? What are the taxing implications on industry? What are the wages paid to Chinese workers doing our farmed-out manufacturing jobs? Are we the people being helped? What happens when the higher paying jobs leave? Where is this all taking us? We saw just a glimpse of the effects when we were trying to get PPE equipment needed for the Corona Virus pandemic.

Today we have many of the conservative political base hanging on to capitalism and denouncing those who are more liberal. They claim the liberals are socialists trying to take from the rich and give to the poor. But not all non-conservatives are that way. I believe that capitalism in a different form can be good. I will call that different form "socially responsible capitalism". Let me explain by sharing a story with you about Milton T. Hershey. Milton was an entrepreneur that invented a way to mass produce chocolate. In 1903 he broke ground to build a new factory in what is now Hershey Pennsylvania. But unlike industrialists then and now, he expanded his vision that would include not only the factory but homes, parks, schools, public transportation, and infrastructure, taking care of and enriching the lives those helping him with his dream. In a sense he shared his wealth with stakeholders and became known as a person of high integrity and profound sense of moral responsibility and benevolence. Health care? Yes, he even built a hospital for the community. Why should we not have that attitude today? Instead, todays owners focus on the short-term bottom line, profits, and money to shareholders that have no interest for anyone but themselves. It is the rule of the systemic patriarchal system. In very few cases to owners now "share" with their stakeholders which include the employees doing the work. This is socially responsible capitalism, a balance between Capitalism and Socialism. This is the model that will help the socioeconomic system to recover. I will also suggest that it is time to bring outsourced manufacturing back to America. If you want to see America the Great, start acting as such. Combine socially responsible capitalism with at home manufacturing and watch our economy and our socioeconomic system blossom.

We are in the year 2020 and it is time we stop, look, and see – be aware that the universe is in a major "self-correcting" mode and it is a chaotic mess. At this point it matters not much if our economic system is Capitalism or Socialism or some other ism. It is in turmoil – boiling over. I am afraid we have seen the rise of the great American Empire, but we are now living and experiencing the fall of the great American Empire. The universe is "self-correcting" to bring the system back into balance. We are literally at the point of decision. What do we want? The ism path we have chosen is not working out. It is too primitive. The situation we are in is not befitting a country with our wealth standing.

So, it does not make much difference what ism path we chose, but we are amid a global reset and it will be one with a new moral order. The universe is demanding it and if you are awake you can feel it. We must awaken to the realization we are physically, mentally, and emotionally living as primitive humans doing instead of enlightened humans being. We are slumbering around living a small fraction of our true power, intelligence, and potential. Our spiritual essence must awaken and save us from this disaster we are living. The Rise of the Divine Feminine is upon us. Some enlightened social-minded capitalists see this and are acting positively. For those who do not, they are driving the bus toward the cliff and the fall of the American empire.

We may not realize it, but we are in the process of establishing an economic system with a new moral order. We do not have a name for this new moral order, but until we do, how about we call it **Socially Responsible Capitalism,** a balance between Capitalism and Socialism where the environment thrives, and there is dignity, respect, and equal rights for all humans. We are God's people that have each other's back, care for and love each other regardless of gender, race, ethnic background, religious preference, or age. W.W.J.D.

IF IT IS TO BE, IT IS UP TO YOU AND ME

Epidemics and Pandemics
Covid -19

2020 and Covid – 19. As of this writing, the outbreak of the
Corona Virus has cast upon the world a hefty energy disturbance
in the human and collective consciousness systems. Millions of
lives have been changed, some temporarily, some permanently.
As of July 13, 2020, over 13 million have been infected and
580,128 lives lost worldwide. Over 3 million have been infected
and 138,000 deaths in just the USA. The troubling news is we are
still in the first wave of the virus spread, so there is great
concern. The effects have been devastating. The economy has
tanked because of shutdowns. Many have either lost their job or
hours have been severely curtailed and those working
"essential" jobs have put their health at risk. Personal finances
have been hit hard and many cannot afford food and are being
threatened with or have been evicted from their homes unable
to pay the rent or mortgage. Schools have been closed upsetting
the learning curves of millions, taxing parents forced to provide
kid sitting and home schooling. The racial disparity in the US has
been further validated, exposing inequities in education (digital
divide – equipment and internet) along with reduced availability
in health care. The current governmental administration has
been slow in response and in some cases, like testing and
tracking, and have been putting out negative signals. This is
causing a tremendous flux in the energy system. Take a moment
and check yourself. Do you have any anxiety, tensions, inner
turmoil, fears, or concerns due the COVID-19?

This section on epidemics and pandemics has been included in
the book because Covid-19 is an extensive part of the energy
disturbance that is elevated by the systemic patriarchal system.
We will explore this in detail. In addition, we will look at past
epidemics and pandemics as comparisons, some of the human

inequities exposed, some good things that come with the downside of the pandemic, and then some solutions. Before we get started, let us start with some definitions.

Epidemics and pandemics: Wikipedia states an epidemic is the rapid spread of disease to a large number of people in a given population within a brief period of time. For example, meningococcal infections, an attack rate in excess of 15 cases per 100,000 people for two consecutive weeks is considered an epidemic. A pandemic is a disease epidemic that has spread across a large region, for instance multiple continents, or worldwide. A widespread endemic disease with a stable number of infected people is not a pandemic.

There is a long listing of epidemics and pandemics going back since the beginning of recorded time. Here is just a sample. A full listing over centuries is available in Wikipedia.

- 1346-1353 - The Bubonic plague, the start of the second plague pandemic hit Europe claimed between 75-200 million lives – estimated 10-60% of the population.
- 1519-1520 - Smallpox in Mexico claimed an estimated 5-8 million lives or 40% of the population.
- 1918-1920 – Spanish flu H1N1 worldwide claimed an estimate 17-100 million lives
- 1968-1970 Hong Kong flu – estimated 1-4 million lives
- 1981-2018 – HIV/AIDS – 32 million + lives lost to date
- 2017-2018 – US seasonal flu – estimated 61,000 lives lost
- 2019 to present (as of July 13, 2020) – Covid-19 – 580,128+ lives worldwide, 138,000+ in USA

It is anyone's guess as to where the final Covid-19 numbers will end, but there are some that say, "this is not so bad", and, "we are overreacting to the pandemic". Others are saying that it is going to get much worse before it gets better. That reality is playing itself out as I write. The biggest concern is the number of deaths and permanent side effects of those who contract the virus.

Here is the thing. Science tells us that if we take preventative action to curtail the spread of the virus, we can avoid the millions of deaths experienced in past pandemics. Statistics show this to be true. Some preventative actions we know that are successful include partial shutdowns, wearing masks, social distancing, and washing hands. Countries other than the Us have been successful in curtailing the spread of Covid-19 using normal standard curtailment protocols – US, not so much. After over 5 months of dealing with the virus, the US is still inadequate in testing, tracing, and shutdowns, and has no federal leadership on the masks and social distancing protocols. Some states are doing well, some not so. What we will explore is the role the systemic patriarchal system plays in all of this.

Let us start with inequities in our social system. Covid-19 has clearly brought to our attention the inequities of our socioeconomic system. We have witnessed glaring examples of COVID spread and impact between the "haves" and "have nots" and racial and ethnic populations. The breakdown in Infections per 10,000 people looks like this. 23 were white, 62 black, and 73 Latino. Black and Latino people are 3X more likely to contract covid-19 as whites. At this writing there are more than 138,000 deaths as a direct result of the virus. There is a disproportionate number of blacks in that number. Blacks, who represent 14% of population accounted for 40% of deaths. Why? Think about the generational effects of substandard housing, limited access to medical treatment, occupation of low paying "essential" jobs, and the need to work. Some other millions lost their jobs, and without income many have already or are in danger of being evicted from or losing their homes. Many are unable to buy food and are getting close to being shut off from unemployment benefits. In addition, for many, there is potential loss of health care.

Educational disparity showed up as another big issue, the digital divide. When schools closed down and went online for teaching, we became acutely aware of the digital divide between the "haves" and "have nots". Home schooling became impossible for many families who did not have access to computers or the internet. For example in Detroit they discovered only 10% in the poor zip codes had access to digital technology – internet and computers. Therefore, only 10% were doing the work. Think of the long-term impact. This is yet another example of the root cause – the systemic patriarchal system – particularly systemic racism that has plagued us for too many years. Check your feelings. How would you feel living in a community where "outsiders" count you out? Remember, nothing can be changed until it is faced. The time is now.

"inequality doesn't just make pandemic viruses worse,
it could cause them" 12 April, Spinney

Relationship between the Systemic patriarchal system and Covid-19:
A virus is a virus. Covid-19 does not care about much, it just is. So, there are two things we need to consider when analyzing viruses and the effects on energy disturbances set up in the world energy system. First, since the virus is just there, what triggers it to suddenly take root in the human body, and second, how can you control the spread once identified?   A number of parameters play into the rooting and then the spread of a virus. The parameters include:
- the state of environment – the level of contamination of our air, water, soil, and vegetation. Is there a petri dish condition where viruses can thrive?
- the health of the individual. people – their immune system which is conditioned by their physical, emotional, mental, and spiritual energy balance; do they get exercise; what do they feed their body -food, beverages

substances, etc.; who they hang out with; family inner circle; and what they feed their mind. It is saddening to note that many of the "have nots" are the ones struggling with obesity, diabetes, and asthma.
- The decisions, mindset, and leadership of those responsible for all the above.

We talked about being in the midst of a perfect storm – an upheaval of the world energy system that is in a self-correction process. The Energy Disturbances Affecting the Collective Consciousness are overwhelming. We have seen the effects of the environmental devastation, wars and conflict, systemic misogyny, systemic racism and ethnic-based discrimination and socioeconomic disparity. The petri dish is ripe with some pretty ugly cultures. So, based on this, we can conclude that Covid-19 has fertile ground to come alive and spread with relative ease. It also suggest that if the energy system is not reversed, we will see a future full of all sorts of epidemics and pandemics … starting with the coming flu season.

So, how do we reduce the incidence and stop the spread of Covid-19, or any unwanted viral concoction? The answer is simple. Take care of ourselves and take care of others. For ourselves that means stay healthy. For care of others that means doing what we know works – wear facial coverings, socially distance, do not touch your eyes, nose, or mouth, and wash your hands frequently, and do not congregate in large groups. Are you taking personal accountability and doing that?

Perhaps the biggest remedy for harnessing COVID and preventing future disasters is have the right decision makers and leaders in place who are tuned into the right processes, procedures, actions, and behaviors necessary to make the "right" most effective decisions. This not only applies to managing Covid-19 but all the other Energy Disturbances Affecting the Collective Consciousness. This requires leadership with a high degree of compassion and social awareness. This is not happening in the current Covid-19 situation.

A snapshot from mid-July 2020 shows the US has the worst corona response in the world. We have problems with testing and contact tracing and lead most all countries in new cases. On July 9, with a combined 2.6 billion population, China, Japan, Korea, Vietnam, Thailand, Malaysia, Indonesia, the Philippines, Australia, and the European Union averaged 6760 new cases, Italy, once a hotspot had less than 200. In the US there were over 60,000 new cases and expected to climb. The current Whitehouse Administration touts what a wonderful job they are doing, testing over 4.5 million per week. Let us see now. With a population of 328 million it will take around 80 weeks to get testing where it needs to be to stop the flow with known protocols. We are now worse than a third world nation in managing our Covid-19 response. Shameful. The current Administrations leadership is reprehensible. We have all the tools we need – the Defense Production Act, the smartest scientists in the world, and a willing population, if lead. Worst of all, there are so many enablers in the ruling party allowing this to continue at the expense of lives. Why do they continue to allow this? Thousands did not need to lose their lives at the expense of an inept administration. Yet the enablers, the "system" continue to enable. I point this out to demonstrate the extent to which the systemic patriarchal system can rise and the damage it can do to society.

The US has become a national humiliation to rest of world. Canada closed its borders to the US. Other countries are looking at closing their borders to an infectious America. We are hearing from outsiders who are saying that once we were a beacon of light and now a total failure. We were once looked upon as leaders in science and democracy in the free world, but we have failed deeply and not just with the COVID situation. Many outsiders and insiders are saying that America has a national leadership problem. The United States is no longer united, and the rest of world is looking on in horror. America has gone to an "us" verses "them" mentality pointing fingers of blame and criticism at others. What we have is a lack of leadership and direction. To me this situation is a glaring example of US leadership being corralled in the systemic patriarchal ideology. The solution, corral and dethrone the systemic patriarchal monarch types that are disrupting our total socioeconomic system and allowing COVID to take hold. It starts with the President and extends to William Barr, Mike Pompeo, Mitch McConnel, and all other enablers of the systemic patriarch types. The "system" is blind to the social needs brought about by the virus.

Congress did pass a rescue package that included an additional $600/week unemployment benefit and freezed lenders and landlords from evictions and foreclosures. That is due to expire August 1. A second rescue package is being negotiated with unbelievable partisanship. The "system", primarily Republicans propose reducing unemployment from $600 to $200. They system enablers want to do this because they claim there is too much incentive for people to remain unemployed. The "system" thinks people should just go back to work. To where? The jobs are gone. They are choosing not to help the people who have no job, are hungry and threatened with eviction, and have lost healthcare. As of August 1, without any action, about 25 million will lose unemployment benefits, and about 40 million could face eviction. The "system" stated their preferences; increase deductions for business meals, reduce funding for testing and tracing, reduce state and school funding, reduce funding for the postal system, slow down the mail to discourage vote by mail, and want to underfund efforts to assure the success of vote by mail in November. As of this writing, the funding of the first rescue package has expired and the Senate has decided to take a long weekend off without any close agreement to try to help the people. It seems that they don't care about the plight of we the people. I can sense some of you thinking this as a political rant, but it is not. I wanted to make the point of showing what the systemic patriarchal system looks like and what it can do and is doing that is having an enormous negative effect on society.

There are those in the "system" that say "open up" without sufficient protocol in place like testing and contact tracing. The "system" says "slow down the testing" knowing that the numbers will look bad for the handling of the situation and have a negative effect on reelection prospects. The "system" (Trump) says "get used to it" like we are supposed to figure out how to live in a burning building. The "system" (Trump) says, "Covid-19 is a left-wing cultural hoax" ... designed hurt him in his reelection process. The "system" (Trump) says, "one day like a miracle it will disappear" without him following what federal guidelines we do have like wearing a mask and social distancing to do his part in curbing the virus. The system (Trump) says "we have to get the schools open. We have to get everything open. A lot of people don't want to do that for political reasons, not for other reasons," and if they don't, he will take away any federal funding. The "system" (Trump) holds political rallies with thousands in attendance without a face mask or social distancing in sight. The "system" enablers are touting "freedom from wearing masks and social distancing" under the title of personal freedoms and rights. There is no law against ignorance, but there is a moral equivalent to be accountable for the effects on fellow humans - especially in light that science has demonstrated the benefits of masks and social distancing. What would ever possess the governor of Georgia to file suit against the mayor and council of Atlanta to negate the face mask mandate? It is pretty simple, do your part! A good question to systemic patriarch types is, do you even care?

Here is the bottom line. There is a direct correlation to cases and deaths associated with Covid-19. Do the math. As of 7/15/20 there were 3,500,000 cases and 138,000 deaths in the US. That is a 3.94% death rate. Now I realize that we have no clue how many cases we actually have since we do little testing. So the percentage is inflated. But one thing is clear. The more cases the more deaths. Let us just look at the increasing incidence of cases. For example, on July 16 there were 73,000 new cases in the US - for just that one day. Instead of using the 3.94% death rate, let us use a more conservative figure of 1%. That means those 73,000 cases will result in 730 deaths ... for just one day. Here is another way to look at it. There are 328 million citizens in the US and 138,000 of us have died due to Covid-19. That is .042% of our population. Is that enough reason to have widespread testing to manage the crisis and for everyone to do their part to stop the spread?

The reality is the "system" does not really care for anything except keep the power and control and getting reelected. Time to take the politics out and install compassionate social-minded leadership.

Something good always comes out of even the worst situations:
There is a tendency in tough times to get caught up and overwhelmed with all the negative "stuff" happening around us and in our world. Yes, we need to do what we can to act toward and manage the pandemic "stuff" the best we can, but at the same time it is always good to pause and lift our minds and focus to the good or positive happening around the pandemic chaos.

First and foremost, the pandemic has caused personal actions that resulted in positive effects on the environment. Air quality was a major benefactor. Planet earth was enjoying the rest resulting from plant closings and lock downs. Satellite observations showed 5- 10% reductions in emissions worldwide, and more over places like China. It was the first time in years that the total span of the Himalayas was visible. Because of reduced travel – fewer vehicle emissions in places like Los Angeles, air quality was significantly improved. Rivers showed signs of clean up, and in Venice, canals became cleaner and clearer. You could actually see the fish, including dolphins enjoying the freshness. It is obvious that shutting things down for a bit allowed the air and creatures of the earth to thrive once again.

To me, one of the most significant positives of the pandemic is "people connecting". There is more "checking in" and "how are you doing" calls, texts, face timing, and messaging with friends and family. There are more private messages on social media sites than before. People are reaching out more than ever to both old and new friends, family members and colleagues. Zoom parties and get togethers have become popular ways to connect. People are genuinely feeling more connected.

Many are rediscovering the outdoors. Bikes and kayaks were sold out at major retail stores. Getting out in the fresh air - hiking, biking, jogging, and walking became major habitual regimens. We are becoming more healthy getting physical exercise.

We cannot say enough about all the heroes who stepped up in response to the pandemic, starting with all the hospital and health care workers and extending to all the "essential" employees who went out of their way in spite of the risk of contracting the virus. Some doctors and nurses traveled thousands of miles to help out in hot spots.

Millions of "acts of kindness" are being performed and range from grocery shopping for those at risk, cooking meals, running errands, pet sitting, and just simply reaching out to help where help is needed. It has been a blessing that shows recognition of the oneness of all and how we are all connected. There are so many more examples of positive benefits of the pandemic and it has become obvious. Shutting things down a bit allowed us to slow down, go inward spiritually, take stock of our lives, and allow the environment to take a fresh breath.

In summary, what we have been talking about are energy disturbances affecting the collective consciousness. Here are a couple takeaways for this section on epidemic sand pandemics. First, although not directly substantiated, there is strong belief of a direct path, a link, between the perfect storm and the spread of viruses. In 2020 that virus is Covid-19. Second, we have shown that a significant factor in the uncontrolled spread of Covid-19, especially the US, is a result of the systemic patriarchal system. And it is clear what we must do.

There was an interesting study comparing the number of daily cases of Covid-19 in Europe and the US. Investigators were trying to understand why Europe seemed to have lower cases per capita than the US. The findings showed there were two main reasons why. First was a lack of national response (leadership), and second, the deluge of misinformation from President Trump and his allies … the "system".

And here is one final interesting note. Many of the countries who have handled COVID well and have it under control … **are run by women!**

Dethrone the Systemic Patriarchal Social System

A New Vision For Leadership

One of my first awakenings about leadership and leadership styles came just after I received my MBA Degree and was working with a headhunter searching for a high-level position in industry. At the time, I particularly liked and was qualified for a position of President and C.E.O. of a small research and development firm. In the process of qualifying me, the headhunter was asking Questions about my background and asked me what my management style was. I answered, Participative Management Style – which in leadership style terms is the "Democratic" style. He said that when interviewing for this position or any other position I should be careful because most industries want "men" with an "Autocratic Style" – managers who are authoritarian, bottom line focused who lead with power, domination, and control. That was the late 70's, but even today, industry is still predominately focused on "get it done, make money for the stockholders – this quarter". I did not see it then, but I do now, we as a society are still operating under the same systemic patriarchal system that has existed for centuries – "capitalistic", "white", "men", "dominant", and "Authoritarian". This is the leadership mold that needs reinvented and a new vision for leadership installed that dismantles the systemic patriarchal system. That is our mission here. Yes, things have been changing slowly but in todays "self-correcting" mode by the universe, we are called to step up, NOW, and aggressively pursue a reset of the consciousness we created.

So, as we look at our dilemma, the first step is to look at what we currently have as leadership style options. As we do, keep in mind some are still appropriate depending on the field of operation, some are not. We will point this out.

Leadership Styles:
A leadership style is a leader's method of management – how they lead, control, direct, implement, and motivate people. This is separate from what they bring to the table such as intellect, knowledge, skills, judgement, creativity, and innovation. Here are the existing predominant styles:

Autocratic: this is a direct and control style. Emphasis is on being directive, somewhat dictatorial, authoritarian, and dominating – get it done style. There is little or no input from subordinates. This style primarily fits and works well in the military field but is often used in teaching and law enforcement fields. We will look at this as one of the potential problems for excessive police force and a training opportunity. We need to be aware that the autocratic style is the predominant style woven into the systemic patriarchal system which is responsible for the imbalance in the world energy system and the chaos we are facing today. We really need to think about "style" when day to day decisions are made and by whom.

Democratic: this style operates on the principle of people involvement – that everyone should have input and play a part in decision making. The practice of social equality is often present, and high involvement teamwork is often used as a tool to success. The results are generally higher productivity and increased morale. This style takes more time for decision making because of the increase in chatter. At times, a democratic style will lead to confused communication and direction, but with a strong manager and a communicated vision it can have greater success and be more effective than one with an autocratic style. This style is particularly suited for the political field, but also for many business and industry applications. I prefer to call this the Participative Management Style.

High Performance Teams: this style is like the democratic style and used when there is a high degree of autonomy in separate work groups with sufficient knowledge and skills. Strong leadership is required. A high degree of trust and social acceptance by each team member is required.

Paternalistic Style: The leader using this style acts as a parental figure who takes care of subordinates as a parent would with a child. The relationship between manager and employee is solid but like the typical parent-child relationship this style is prone toward disruption when the child wants to act on their own with their own ideas.

Laissez-Faire Style: this is a "free range" style where the rights and power for making decisions is fully given to the subordinate. It requires self-motivated, knowledgeable, and talented employees.

Narcissistic Style: This is the dictatorship style. The individual is a vain, self-absorbed, egotistical, selfish, and self-important. "Do it my way or else". You always must be careful of the what else. This style has had a prominent role in the systemic patriarchal system we created. The consciousness of this style needs eradicated.

As the universe self-corrects and we experience chaos and dynamics that go along with it, just remember, we are getting thrown back at us exactly what we programmed into the collective consciousness. That includes the environmental devastation, world conflicts, systemic misogyny, systemic racism, socioeconomic disparity, and pandemics. Our world energy system is totally out of balance. Recognize though that most of what we are seeing is the result of our forefathers embracing a patriarchal social system that has festered into a systemic monstrosity. But here is the deal. With the right consciousness, the right decisions, the right action, and with a new leadership vision, we can and will turn this ship around quickly – if we put our minds to it.

So, we pause now and look at what we have and ask the questions. What do we want, what needs to change? Who should do it? What kind of leaders and leadership styles do we need to move toward to replace what has not worked – the systemic patriarchal system we now have. Regardless of whether the field of usage is political, business, industry, or the military, what is the common ground we should pursue to make it work? What kind of consciousness makes it work for all? The realization must come that the qualities of the Divine Feminine must be infused into leaders.

Here is a unique thought. Why not emulate what female leaders bring to the table whether in business, family, or spiritual situations. They have been enormously successful. I would like to validate that statement by paraphrasing a comment made by Barak Obama in an interview with the BBC in December 2019 … that women are indisputably better leaders than men, and if matters were run by women, living standards would improve. Why not start a leadership transformation with all the women making the decisions. Up until now all the men made the decisions and how has that worked out? Okay, this is interesting thinking, but what we will be attempting to do is a bring the balance of energy to the system. The message though is that women naturally express the qualities of the Divine Feminine and extend this to the human experience. So, what are we looking for? Simply, we need leaders who lift people up to be their best, not leaders that dominate with power, fear, and exclusion. We need leaders that lead with compassion, empathy, and inclusion.

I have always believed that the sign of a good leader is one who has a superior vision of the organization and has the skills and ability to connect with, communicate with and motivate others to carry out the vision while being socially (and spiritually) conscious of the needs of all parties – employees, customers, and other stakeholders. In my consulting business, I have experienced that this is the best way to achieve sustainable success while balancing all resources. This is a true democratic process. If you look at leadership from this perspective, you see it parallels the spiritual values we have been discussing and is comprised of both the divine feminine and divine masculine. It is ONE. Transformational Leadership is unifying leadership.

What our world needs is a leadership style that fits the situation but Is infused with compassion, understanding, and empathy – a social consciousness that balances the energy forces. But a start will be getting rid of the highly integrated systemic systems and people that got us into this mess. Replace the people and systems with those who have the right mind, the right heart, and the right skills and can make the decisions that will bring balance to the world.

Our society is at the tipping point where our systemic patriarchal system is being challenged. Our challenge is to have gender equality as a foundation for a peaceful, prosperous, and sustainable world. In addition, equal access to education, health care, decent work and real political representation is a must. We know what dependence and independent look like, and that does not work. We must Learn how to be interdependent. We need to get connected to and stay connected to all our brothers and sisters. After all we are already ONE.

What it all comes down to is how we make our choices and decision. If we all encompassed value driven decisions that embodied connectivity, empathy, compassion, and understanding – a "we" versus "them" attitude, our unity, our oneness will transform society. What we are doing is creating a completely new paradigm, and as we believe and act so it will be. Keep in mind it will include the interdependency of both genders, a balance of both the divine feminine and the divine masculine. We know that consciousness is energy and when we put a consistently act in a positive vein, with the collective energy of everyone coming together as ONE, our world, our systems, our people, our collective consciousness will be transformed.

The New Vision For Leadership

What I am proposing here is adding a new category of leadership style. Presenting:

> <u>Social Consciousness</u> **Leadership Style:** this is a leadership style that uses any of the traditional leadership styles - Autocratic, Democratic, or High Involvement Teams, whichever best suits the situation and field of operation – BUT - does so with a social consciousness that embraces compassion, empathy, and understanding.

Leadership With a Social Consciousness

Decision 2020
Acting in an Era of Change

We are amid elevated levels of social unrest, climate change, and volatility in the world economy. Protests and demonstrations are increasing over issues of inclusion, equality, and equity. And, with the lynching of George Floyd, systemic racism has brought a mandate demanding transformation of our culture. The stress and uncertainty of this social upheaval is causing changes in our lives we are uncertain and stressed about, not prepared for, and bringing concerns for our uncertain future. Reading this book up to this point you are aware of what is happening. The world, the universe is self-correcting, trying to correct the huge imbalance in the world energy system which has darkened the collective consciousness. Just know there is a "seismic shift" taking place in our lives, our world, and the human/collective consciousness.

What we need to realize is that the turmoil we are working through is the result of our transition to the third phase of the evolution of the world social system. As pointed out by Mike Dooley in Notes From the Universe, we have progressed from a **primitive society** and lived by the rule of might ... the strong prevailed. Then we moved on to a more **advanced society** where we lived by the rule of law ... and the privileged prevailed. This has been a 400-year evolutional process and brings us to where we are today with a systemic patriarchal System still ruling. The third phase we are moving into is the **enlightened society** phase where we are to live by the rule of love ... where everyone is a contributor and shares in the rewards of life and the economic system. So, as we progress, keep in mind that what we are experiencing in our world today is the result of the transition from phase two to phase three. Transitions always tend to be messy, chaotic, and seemingly disruptive, so buckle your seat belt.

As we make the transition to and enlightened society realize we are witnessing the consequences of our past choices. Some of these were good and some not so good, but we are at a point of choice about the future our world. The choices are, allow this energy imbalance to continue and escalate and potentially result in the sixth mass extinction of our world – or – take appropriate action to reverse the cycle to bring back peace and respect for the sacredness of the earth and each and every life which is the enlightened society. I hope the choice is obvious for you. Being an optimist by nature, I know this can and will be done. Yes, this will be a difficult and an enormous undertaking to bring together people of diverse cultures, nations, beliefs, and backgrounds. It will take a commitment by each of us, individually and collectively. The reason I see this happening is because I see an awakening of the people of the world to who we truly are - Spirit beings called to act in the oneness of our nature. This is a spiritual revolution … the rise of the Divine Feminine AND Divine Masculine as one. We all need to move forward with active engagement and rigorous self-education.

In the end, what we are calling for is a radical change, a seismic shift in human/collective consciousness which was built on a systemic patriarchal system, to one that has an environmental and social consciousness. This will be a shift from a system of power, control, and dominance by a few "men", to a system of power of and by a diverse society of all people, driven by a spiritual base of love, compassion, empathy, and service. This is necessary to transition to a phase three, "enlightened society".

In the Forward of this book we presented the tribulation we are going through in the form of the Perfect Storm. So, if we want to talk about what decisions and actions we need to take to reverse the cycle, we need to address the specific areas causing the energy imbalances. Here again is the specifics of what we are dealing with:

The Perfect Storm

Climate crises
Covid-19 Pandemic
Systemic racism – civil unrest at a high
Systemic misogyny – being called out
Discriminatory practices being challenged – human
rights for women, blacks,
      LGBTQ communities, and minorities – all
      those being disenfranchised
Fight against voter suppression and oppression
Political disfunction – polarization; lack of
      Administrative and Congressional
      leadership
Socioeconomic disparity causing major societal
      disturbances.
Economic recession
Waring conflicts and nuclear threats
Healthcare crises
Moral and spiritual deterioration
Systemic patriarchal system – power, dominance, and
      control causing major distresses; approaching
      pure fascism by some

Decision 2020 – what does that mean? It means that we are at the tipping point and we have some decisions and choices to make to help us through and lift us above the "perfect storm". If we want to be successful in turning this around, we must awaken. We must realize and be aware of this simple truth, **we are what we think**. The storm? We did this to ourselves by our "thoughts", decisions, choices, and actions in the past. Likewise, our future - what we will become, is predicated on the predominant "thoughts", decisions, and choices of the total of the collective consciousness of we the people today. We are determining the fate of the nation and the world NOW, today. Pause for a moment and let this sink in. We are deciding what we will have, and what we will be – in this present moment. That is a bit scary but extremely exciting. Knowing and acting on this knowledge puts us in a position of being intentional visionaries and cocreators of a changed, positive, and bright future. Indeed, 2020 is the year of decision. If we want to be transformed to an enlightened society, now is the time to act. You know, we the American people are the ultimate judges and the ultimate decision makers of our fate. Are you ready to rumble? If So:

> **Vision, think, choose, decide, and act for an enlightened society. Organize, protest, sit-in, stand up, and vote for your vision. Be positive and constructive - not destructive**

Okay, so we need a solid transition action plan. But before we jump in, we need to first have a quick review of why we are where we are. Change can only come by identify and knowing the behaviors we want to eliminate. We have awakened to the underlying problem behind a trashed environment, systemic racism, exclusion of women in all facets of life, socioeconomic disparity, and waring conflicts. It all started centuries ago when our fate was sealed by a conscious and unconscious choice of embracing a primitive and then a patriarchal social system. Today we are witnessing the consequences of allowing these choices to fester into an uncontrollable systemic monstrosity. The universe has awakened us that a change is necessary – or else.

For our action plan, the first order of business is focus on the coming November elections and what action we can all take to insure that 2020 is the year that we jump-start a positive seismic shift in our social consciousness system. This will be a movement that will carry us to the November elections and beyond. The momentum must be continuous and self-sustaining. This is a monumental time in our history to show up and be counted.

For the November 2020 elections and beyond we must keep in mind that our policies, laws, procedures, and practices are carried out by people – people that you and I select to represent we the people. So, we must know and select the right people – people with the right mind, the right heart, and the right soul. These will be people with intelligence, compassion, understanding, and empathy - people who are real leaders. The way to look at our action plan is to decide and choose who we want to lead us out of the disorders of the perfect storm we find ourselves in. Remember, what we are doing is changing the system. We want a shift from a system operated by the power of the few old systemic patriarchal monarchs, to a system of enlightenment driven by the power of the people. So, let us look at some specifics:

- **The Environment**: support, sponsor, endorse, and fund candidates who believe "the science" and have an enlightened knowledge and vision of what needs to be done to slow and reverse the effects of global warming. These candidates will have campaign plans that include leadership for pulling together the forces and resources of all world leaders to develop and enact policies, laws, and plans to save the environment.

- **Voter suppression**: put pressure on and remove high-level old school systemic patriarchs including the President, Attorney General and Senate Majority Leader plus other administrative enablers that are deviously plotting to repress votes. Choose the right people to expose and eliminate gerrymandering.
- **Vote by mail**: make it happen. Remember the headlines and quotes; "Trump ramps up attack on mail-in voting", and, "Trump puts crony in the position of Postmaster General to slow down the mail …" and, "if we allowed mail-in ballots I would surely lose the election". Organize, protest, sit-in, stand up, vote
- **Racism – racial injustice**: be adamant about police and justice department reform. Vote out the people, policy, and laws that continue to allow systemic racism to

flourish. Vote in the people, policy and laws that get it done. Force candidates to include these initiatives in their platforms. Organize, protest, sit-in, stand up, vote

- **Human rights inequities:** vote for the candidates who pledge initiating policies, procedures, practices, and laws that eliminate the divide in education, housing, income, and healthcare opportunities plaguing blacks, low income, and minority families.
- **Health Care:** support, sponsor, endorse, and fund candidates who believe that health care for all people is a fundamental requirement for a healthy enlightened society and should be provided regardless.
- **Socioeconomic disparity.** Vote in the candidates who advocate shifting more funds from war toys to social systems, who advocate drastically increasing the minimum wage, refundable tax credits, changing the tax system to better benefit low income citizens, and increase taxes on corporations and the wealthy.
- The Current President is the greatest agent of chaos. Vote him out.
- **Women as equal partners in the political arena**: Give everyone an equal chance to compete fairly based on skills and talents; see women as good as or potentially even better decision makers because of their inherent nature. Vote women into office, balance the feminine/masculine energy of those who lead us.
- **Legislative process**: Big money is influencing and corrupting the legislative and electoral process. Vote for candidates on record to eliminate large corporate contributions to campaigns of elected officials and are in favor of reducing/eliminating the ability of lobbyists to dictate/influence the workings of the legislative process (like the NRA and big pharma). Time to establish term limits for elected officials.

- **Pandemics:** support candidates and an administration who can lead in a crisis, who believe and act on the recommendations of science.
- Vote for pro-immigration advocates that believe in a fair and just immigration process.
- Socially responsible capitalists: vote in candidates that understand what this is ... breaking the cycle of systemic patriarchal monarch types. Level the socioeconomic playing field.

Who and what not to vote for:
- Vote NO for candidates that are dictatorial and insult everyone, going after anyone, and belittling everyone who threatens them.
- Vote NO for someone who has a long track record of making disgusting and demeaning statements about women and anyone they feel is a threat.
- Vote NO for someone who makes statements such as – "no Medicare for all as long as I am the Majority Leader", and "we need to completely eliminate and repeal the ACA" without having a better plan
- Vote NO for someone who makes statements such as: "slow down the testing, it is increasing the number of known Covid-19 cases".
- Vote NO for someone who legislates with a totally partisan view of "it's us versus them" mentality. As Trump said about protesters, "these are not my people, these are not my voters."
- Vote out a Senate Majority leader whose partisan politics has shelved hundreds of bills that could have potentially advanced our social system.
- Vote NO for anyone whose first choice is doubling down on militaristic resolution to domestic or foreign conflict rather than de-escalation and resolution through listening and understanding.

- Vote NO for someone who invites foreign intervention in the election process to win.
- Vote NO for someone who Is more in love with their power than their love and compassion for the people.
- Vote NO for those who use fear rhetoric as a tactic to scare you into voting for them

"When outward displays of ignorance and selfishness become Political statements, it might be time to rethink your politics"

unknown

Who and what to vote for:
- Vote yes for candidates and party that has a solid plan to heal the country
- Return competent, compassionate, and loyal leadership to the White House
- Restore US Global Leadership
- Aggressively pursue racial and economic disparity programs that can heal the country. The Senate must be flipped to do so.
- Vote for candidates that bring moral leadership, integrity, passion, and empathy to the table
- Vote for candidates, issues, laws, and policies that are approached on a bipartisan basis
- Vote for candidates who listen to and act on the messages of civil and social unrest.
- Vote for candidates who campaign to eliminate educational inequities. They will have a campaign platform to develop laws, policies and practices that work for equal opportunity access to learning including buildings and equipment, technical tools, and internet access.
- Vote for candidates who see through the systemic patriarchal racist and power grabbing system and are taking steps to usher in the enlightened society

- Vote for candidates who are servants and do the work of the people, not themselves and the big corporate dollar.
- Hold the biggest protest at the ballot box on election day.

2020 is the year that we jump-start a positive seismic shift in our social consciousness system. This will be a movement that will carry us to the November elections and beyond. After the election, the momentum must be continuous and self-sustaining. This is a monumental time in our history to show up and be counted.

The systemic patriarchal system has been with us for hundreds of years and there is much work to do to assure transition to a new enlightened society. Let us use the momentum of this 2020 jump start of the November elections to give us the courage to sustain our effort to clean up the mess of the perfect storm. Remember the successes and the motto – **Organize, protest, sit-in, stand up, and vote. Be positive and constructive - not destructive.** There is still plenty of work to be done.

Acting in the interests of others defines character. Acting in one's self-interest requires zero character. It is no longer about being a Democrat or Republican, It is about saving the environment and respect, dignity, and equal rights for all humanity!

Act as if your life and the life of the planet depends on it because it does

The Goal - Dethrone the Systemic Patriarchal Social System

All In - Together

The year is 2020 and we find ourselves in the midst of battling the "Perfect Storm" that has been raging, seemingly out of control. The dark night of climate change, Covid-19, systemic misogyny, systemic racism, broad based discrimination, socioeconomic disparity, healthcare crises, moral and spiritual deterioration has caught our attention and awakened us to the Universe speaking in the form of an energy self-correction. As Einstein noted on many occasions, the Universe broadcasts ideas for its well-being all the time. This time it is rather pronounced. Our awakening has inspired a global movement to change a broken system. As stated by Rev. William J. Barber II, "we are called to be a movement." We are on a hero's journey through challenges facing us. We are in a battle for the soul of America. And so it is.

It would be helpful to have a big picture perspective of where we are and what we need to do in this time of seismic change. One of the best organizations that does this kind of thing is Humanity's Team. They are progressive visionaries who do extensive research, communications, training and development, and coaching. Their team consists of many leading spiritual thinkers that are tuned into what is happening today. Here is an explanation I received from Steve Farrell of Humanity's Team. His view is that we are living from an unconscious pattern of living on the Earth and must shift to a conscious design and an elevated humanity supporting the well-being and balance for all living species. This is the awakening I write about. Steve noted that our way of living on Earth is not sustainable - we've lost our sense of cohesion with nature, the Divine, and life. Collectively, we've been barreling down a dangerous path toward a future that leaves our children and future generation very exposed. The current awakening and shift that is occurring is bringing humanity to another level of being. He is asking that we be aware of this spiritual awakening and re-imagine our role in this, and place all of our energy at its disposal. His insight is we are evolving to Homo Universalis. He believes evolution is calling the entire world to this place – humanity, the animal kingdom and the Earth. "Evolution has a certain destination and cannot be stopped once it reaches a particular momentum state". This is the reset I talk about. To me, that is something to get excited about.

Continuing on a positive note, our struggle, pain, and suffering is a wake-up call. The challenges we face as a society have become an internal motivating mechanism for many to find their voices and express them in unique forms. With protests and sit-ins we have become empowered to take action to make needed changes that move us toward saving the environment to gaining respect, dignity, and equal rights for all humanity. Perhaps you today are among the masses looking for ways to contribute to the reshaping of the world. Until this moment we have been crawling along making a few adjustments to the system but now we feel an urgency to make a seismic shift in the systems that have been holding us back from receiving our good. We should not fear or be threatened by all this, we should embrace the discomfort with the realization that this is just the Universe speaking to us with a loud voice that we are in a Global reset. It is an energy self-correcting process, and it is a spiritual journey. We are called to GO ALL IN. As you do you will realize this as an extraordinary moment to be alive. Out of all the hundreds and thousands of years of cultural evolution we are at the greatest turning point in the history of civilization. There is a reason you were born at this time in history. You were chosen to be a part of it. In these days and these times, your light is needed more than ever.

"Do not be dismayed by the brokenness of the world. All things break. And all things can be mended. Not with time, as they say, but with intention. So go. Love intentionally, extravagantly,

unconditionally. The broken world waits in darkness for the light that is you."

R. Knost

"Do not be daunted by the enormity of the world's grief. Do justly now, love mercy now, walk humbly now. You are not obligated to complete the work, but neither are you free to abandon it."

The Talmud

As we become involved in the transition from a primitive society to an enlightened society, we need to take caution to stay away from the blame game. A good portion of the population have been Trump bashing because of his policy decisions, radical behavior, ego centered tweet wars with those he does not like, the need for control, power, and using military force as the answer to domestic conflict. But in the illusionary reality we live in, this is just behavior that has been normalized in our society over hundreds of years. The thing is we did not even realize what was going on. We were unaware that we are unaware. It did not start with Trump, The existing Congress, or industrialists, but it has come to an intensified pitch. The normalized behaviors of the systemic patriarchal system have become ugly and one-sided, manifesting the systemic racism, misogyny, bigotry, racial and gender inequality, and white nationalism at its worst. Yes, we have made progress, but the "leaders" of the patriarchal system sense action against them and are stepping up their initiative to keep its power and control in place. This is a major cause behind the "perfect storm". But we are awakening and calling forth a seismic shift in culture and consciousness. This is a change backed by the entire nation and the world.

The major awakening started with our government's handling of the Corona Virus and peaked with the current civil unrest following George Floyds death. This civil unrest – the protests, were joined and supported by all of God's children – people of all colors and ethnicities, men, women, children, that have proclaimed that enough is enough. People are sick of generational poverty, sick of structural racism and misogyny, and sick of the status quo. ENOUGH! There is a seismic awakening and a call to action.

The first step We talked about is to vote - remove from office and retire all the staunch supporters of the existing systemic patriarch monarch types. That includes Trump, McConnell, Barr, and all their enablers in both the House and Senate whether Republican or Democrat. The "system" built the swamp and it is owned by special interest groups. There needs to be a house cleaning from top to bottom in the Whitehouse, Congress, State Houses, and local Councils. They need to be replaced by candidates that have the new vision for leadership and possess a balanced feminine/masculine energy with a sense of compassion, empathy, and understanding. It is about making the right decisions with leaders that have the right skills, the right minds, and the right hearts. It is about creating a new dawn for the environment with respect, dignity, and equal rights for all humanity. It is about bringing the system back into balance.

The transition to an enlightened society begins with all of us. It begins with the level of our thinking – having the right mind. When "we" as a collective consciousness come together with the right think – behave – act mentality, critical mass will be reached, and we will "see" the transformation from our systemic patriarchal system to an enlightened society. It is possible and can be done relatively quickly – if we choose so.

I would like to share an example of consciousness and awakening that I borrowed from my Genesis 2.0 book. This example holds the secret to life and living together in peace. I call it ...

The Parable of the Symphony Orchestra

And the wise man said: "Let us look at the people of the world today - a collection of extraordinary points of light or energy with enormous potential, talents, skills, and values - all highly resilient overcomers. That is who we are, expressions of that light. We are all UNDERLINE ONE - it is all energy - a continuous expression of God - integral part of Pure Consciousness, just like the components and composition of a symphony orchestra. But you say, why don't we see it and feel it? The answer is because we are asleep and hypnotized and not awake to the reality of who we really are - our spiritual essence. We have chosen the illusion of separateness by focusing on our differences, race, color, religion, beliefs, male-female, politics, socioeconomic status, and so on. We fail to see the unity and oneness in front of our eyes. We were put on this planet as one huge symphony orchestra - BUT - we are all doing our separate things, thinking individually that we each are the best, that it is my way or the highway. The string section is fighting with the brass; the percussion section is clanging and gonging, not in sequence or rhythm with anything. The piano, harp and base are off in lala land, and the conductor is trying to make order out of the chaos. Do you get the visual? Now, think of the best symphony orchestra you have ever heard; maybe 100 to 150 members, 20 or more different instruments, and a world class conductor that has remarkably made order out of potential chaos. Think about the energy/vibration of the instruments brought together by an attitude of unity, oneness and purpose using their uniqueness, talents, and skills. They have all agreed on the music composition, written for the strength of their "different" instruments. During some of the more dynamic movements in a piece, the audience can "feel" the shimmering effervescence of the harmonious vibrations produced by such an orchestra, and it can give you the shivers. So, what do we need to do to the symphony orchestra of our world today to get the peace and harmony we desire? With this parable, the answer is obvious: First, awaken and become aware of who we are – see Appendix B. Next, identify your uniqueness, skills, and talents ...your strengths, AND then, accept and promote the differences, uniqueness, skills, and talents of your "brother", and finally, make a choice - DECIDE or choose to "play together" the symphony of the Master. It is time we look at the qualities of each person we encounter, what makes them distinct, the gifts they bring to the orchestra and become intrigued with and embrace what they offer the world. It must be a conscious effort - an elevation of your consciousness which rearranges your perception of the world in which you live - and making a "real" connection with others without prejudice or bias. As Stephen Covey said, (in our world) "strength lies in differences, not in similarities". But where it really counts is on the spiritual side. We are all alike inside, and the biggest of all similarities, we all possess the same DNA of Spirit. Consider: God is Spirit, God is Love, we are Spirit, we are Love, Love is the symphony. Imagine the music we can – we will make - together.

We are all musical instruments, manifestation machines. Our thoughts, sounds, words, and actions (all vibrations) go into the collective consciousness and return as a symphony. Our world will awaken to the power of our inner Spirit and come together when we see beyond the illusion of our ego-based consciousness to accept and understand the uniqueness and strengths of others and act accordingly. It is time we awaken and realize that we still live in a primitive world that wages wars and partakes in horrific injustices to each other out of our primal fears, greed, and prejudices about those that are "different" than us. It is well time for the transformation from a primitive to an enlightened society.

"The Lord did not people the earth with a vibrant orchestra of personalities only to value the piccolos of the world. Every instrument is precious and adds to the complex beauty of the symphony."
Joseph B. Wirthlin

"I am sure that we would differ less and clasp our hands in friendliness. Our thoughts would pleasantly agree If I knew you and you knew me."
Nixon Waterman, "In a Merry Mood"

To play in the world symphony we must Get over the them – me attitude. There is only "We" - "WE" as "ONE" orchestrating movement - One Spirit, One Tribe, Many Stories. We are all equally valued and important expressions of God.

One of the situations that helped me "see things differently" - to get a true perspective, was listening to the message of Edgar Mitchel during his Apollo 14 moon mission. I call it the 240,000-mile view or perspective. At 240,000 miles away, he describes the earth as a ball he could hold in one hand. As the earth nestled in his outstretched hand, he describes the feeling of love, peace, and harmony. He saw things as one harmonious unit. If you can envision that, it is a true beginning to healing the earth and its people.

OK. So where does awakening start? It starts knowing who you are – with an awareness that we are spiritual beings having a human experience, not the opposite. As part of the "who am I" exercise in my seminars, I love to ask the question, "what part of you is spirit and what part physical?" The answers vary all over the spectrum, but we have learned about the different states of existence and know it is all energy, and we are part of that energy system. Therefore, we are 100% Spirit – manifest in human form, and possess the unique power of Spirit to do awesome things. However, we often live our lives totally wrapped up in the junk and "sinfulness" of our human experiences, not realizing, not being aware, and totally ignoring or ignorant of the truth and power of our God/Spirit/Self. We allow the illusions of the world, mostly by default, to trap and imprison us in the human "dream" state. Here is the scoop: we actually live within the Spiritual State. It is part of the Energy System, and we will experience it only to the degree that we are open to and conscious of Spirit in our lives. We just know it and act accordingly. When this happens, chaos and confusion are subdued. When our talk, our conversations, our focus, and our actions are centered in Spirit, we will experience heaven on earth. Ernest Holmes writes:

> *"Humankind does not face an eternal struggle against some external force that desires our downfall The only struggle, the only battle, the only thing that needs to be overcome is our own ignorance, our own lack of awareness and recognition of the beneficent Power and creativity that is the source of all things."*

Here is a must realization: every person is as much an expression of God as I am. We are all spirits of the ONE. When you look in anyone's eyes use your spiritual eyes and see the oneness in theirs. "See" how much we are alike, not how much we are different. Then shape your thoughts, words, and actions accordingly. This attitude automatically realigns your energy and the result is the reshaping of the collective consciousness. At the same time, a new consciousness will bring about correction of the injustices that have occurred for hundreds of years. Got to trust and just do it. Have the 240,000-mile perspective. Have the vision.

Did you know you subconsciously repeat 60,000 – 80,000 words and thought-patterns each day? And, that the words you're thinking and saying directly influence your health and your future? So, do you want a new world that works for everyone? Then where is your mind? Remember, When we collaborate with Spirit and believe – when we have the vision, when we act and behave accordingly, we will not only "see" but be that new world. Realize that with every thought, word, belief, and action we are creating our future. It is like writing a new book or shooting a new movie, only we are the authors and producers. Let's get it right. Remember, everything is spiritual. Everything comes from the invisible spiritual realm to the physical. We therefore need to connect with Spirit. The future is in our hands, so we must envision, imagine, act, and believe for one day we will be in the place we want to be. We can overcome great odds

In the words of Ernest Holmes:

> *"We are the chemists in the laboratory of the infinite; what shall we produce"*

On July 4, we celebrate Independence Day. This year, 2020 I was imagining back what it must have been like 244 years ago with the protests, revolution, and the fight to overcome the tyranny of British Rule. We were fighting for liberty, freedom, courage, independence, and choice. And now today, we are fighting for the same things, but it is against the tyranny of the systemic patriarchal system. Yes, on July 4 we celebrate our freedom, but there are so many of our citizens who "still" have not experienced true freedom. The oppression of the systemic system has kept them in bondage. This is a cause worth fighting for

If you want a vision of what our world can be, I encourage you to read and listen to the lyrics of two patriotic songs about America – God Bless America, and America The Beautiful. Sweet dreams are made of this. To achieve this vision we must transform our culture to one of an enlightened society. That means creating a new paradigm - a belief system of an enlightened society. When we change the paradigm, the world changes for us, and our response to the world also changes. The old adage is true. If you do not like the world you see, change it. You can experience and respond to it differently by creating a new paradigm – a new vision, a new belief, a new culture. What we are in the process of doing is making a seismic shift in our personal and collective worldview. To keep this a sustainable process we need awakened from our imbedded thought patterns, educated out of our ignorance, and continually exposed to new creative ideas and solutions.

"The world as we have created it is a process of our thinking. It cannot be changed without changing our thinking."
Albert Einstein

"Do not be conformed to this world, but be transformed by the renewal of your mind, that by testing you may discern what is the will of God, what is good and acceptable and perfect.
Romans 12:2 ESV

One of my favorite philosophers – spiritual icons is the late Peace Pilgrim. She taught and lived a life of love and believed and taught the oneness and universal order of all things. She spoke of an impending awakening or a transformation to what was presented in this book as a transformation from a primitive to an enlightened society. She saw this as a spiritual awakening where we know and live the truth that we are all ONE in God, one in Spirit, and if we live this truth, peace will prevail. I agree with her wholeheartedly and it is one of the reasons I have developed a personal mission *of "Helping individuals and organizations awaken to and fully live their spiritual essence".* Here is a quote from Peace Pilgrim stating her strong belief:

"We are merging into a euphoria of absolute unity with all of life; with humanity, with the creatures of the Earth, the trees and plants, the air, the water. This God-centered nature is constantly awaiting to govern our life gloriously. We have the free will either to allow it to govern our life or not. The choice is always ours."

It is important to remember that the chaos we "see" in the world does not have to be. We are seeing it because of past choices. It is our thinking that has made it so. The key to change and transformation to an enlightened society is to lift our thinking to a higher order - to envision, think, believe, behave, and act accordingly. It is as simple as that, but the process will not necessarily be easy. We must keep our eyes on the prize as noted by Peace Pilgrim. I like to explain things in terms of energy, so my take on what we are doing is returning to living in rhythm with each other and the Earth.

"The soul, being the seat of memory, already contains a record of everything that ha ever happened to us. …The sum total of all erroneous human belief binds until the individual mentally lifts himself above the law of averages into the higher law of Spiritual Individualism." Ernest Holmes

And finally, I want to share some words of wisdom from one of my favorite spiritual authors Richard Rohr. It will be a quote from his book "Yes, AND…". On page 133 he talks about Spiritual Globalization. It is a message about coming together in "oneness" and if not, the consequences.

> *What we have in common is that we are all breathing the same air, relying upon the same Brother Sun and walking on the same Mother Earth. That is the common collective. That gives us the power to read reality with foundational truth, beyond any ideology. We are first and foremost and universally members of the one earth community (Ephesians 4:4-6 surely intuited this). But we are able to do this now, as in no other period of history. It is forced upon us now because we know that if we keep following this artificial separation and over-individuation, my rights over common good, the whole thing is over in a century or so.*

I do not believe any of us wants it to be over. We have the power of choice to make the changes necessary to make the seismic shift in consciousness and move from a primitive society to an enlightened society. This is a spiritual journey that we are all called to and should look forward to. We are resetting our social consciousness system and rebuilding the infrastructure that will carry us into a bright future. Our decisions and choices today will act as the cause that will generate the effect we desire. Do not be discouraged and consciously chose to create a world that works for everyone.

The power of God within us is like a sleeping giant which must be awakened that it may spring into action".
Ernest Holmes, "This Thing Called Life"

In the words of John Lewis:

"Get into Good Trouble – Keep moving"

We Need To Be All In
Together in Oneness

Biography

DANIEL PAUL WOODRING

Daniel Paul Woodring is a Minister, Author, Spiritual Advisor, Chaplain, and Certified Life Coach. He is the Spiritual Director of the Center for Spiritual Growth and Awakening – an organization with a stated mission of "Helping Individuals and Organizations Awaken to and Live Their Spiritual Essence".

Daniel has combined over 30 years of business and management experience in the Utility Industry with advanced academic credentials in strategy formulation, leadership, and team building.   He served 13 years as President and Managing Director of **Performance Plus Technologies**, an Organizational Consulting Firm in Cincinnati, Ohio. For the last 10 years, Daniel has focused his energy on the Spirituality and Ministerial fields.

As a Spiritual Coach, Personal Life Coach and Professional Coach, Daniel has helped thousands with his book *"No Regrets, a Comprehensive Guide and Workbook for Mapping Your Life's Journey – Regardless of Age"* published in 2003.

In addition to being an ordained minister, Daniel holds a bachelor's degree in Mechanical Engineering, a master's degree in Business Administration, and a Master of Chaplaincy Studies. His ministerial, management, and consulting background is extensive and include certifications as a Life Coach and Business Coach. He has served as coach and consultant to a variety of individuals and businesses.

Daniel also served on the Faculty of the University of Phoenix, Cincinnati, teaching Critical Thinking - Applied Problem Solving and Decision Making, and Organizational Behavior.

www.ingramcontent.com/pod-product-compliance
Lightning Source LLC
Chambersburg PA
CBHW032115280326
41933CB00009B/850